THE EPIC POISE

THE EPIC POISE

A CELEBRATION OF
Ted Hughes

edited by
NICK GAMMAGE

faber and faber

First published in 1999
by Faber and Faber Limited
3 Queen Square London WC1N 3AU

Photoset by Parker Typesetting Service, Leicester
Printed in England by Clays Ltd, St Ives plc

Nick Gammage is hereby identified as editor
of this work in accordance with Section 77
of the Copyright, Designs and Patents Act 1988

A CIP record for this book
is available from the British Library

ISBN 0-571-19686-1

2 4 6 8 10 9 7 5 3 1

For Carol, Frieda and Nicholas
and in memory of Ted

All this, too, is stitched into the torn richness,
The epic poise
That holds him so steady in his wounds, so loyal to his doom,
    so patient
In the machinery of heaven.

from 'October Salmon'

Contents

Editor's Note xiii

PART ONE: On the Poetry and Prose of Ted Hughes

Poetry From Cambridge 1952–54 KARL MILLER 3

The Hawk in the Rain
Ted Hughes and The Hawk in the Rain ADAM THORPE 7
'Wind' LINDSAY CLARKE 11

Lupercal
Lupercal ALAN GOULD 15
Notes on a Footnote JAMES LASDUN 18

Wodwo
Wodwo BLAKE MORRISON 23
'Full Moon and Little Frieda' ANDREW MOTION 31
Journeying to 'Sunday' MARTIN BOOTH 33
'Pibroch' W. S. MERWIN 38
Hurrying through the Underworld: 'Second Glance at a
    Jaguar' JAMIE MCKENDRICK 42
'Gnat-Psalm' PETER REDGROVE 47

The Iron Man and Moon-Bells
The Iron Man and the 'Moon-Hops' WENDY COPE 52
Moon-Bells SUSAN HILL 55

[ix]

Crow
    Omen and Amen: On 'Littleblood' SEAMUS HEANEY 59
    Crow: A Reading D. J. ENRIGHT 62
    Six Crows LEONARD BASKIN 65

Season Songs
    'A Cranefly in September' BRIAN PATTEN 71

Moortown and *River*
    'Tractor' RAYMOND BRIGGS 73
    'New Year exhilaration' ROGER MCGOUGH 77
    Moortown and *River* LACHLAN MACKINNON 79
    'The Gulkana': Recognizing Home NICK GAMMAGE 82
    Moortimes MEDBH MCGUCKIAN 92

Prometheus on his Crag
    'The black day splits with lightning' FRED RUE JACOBS 99

Gaudete
    Discovering *Gaudete* SIMON ARMITAGE 103

Remains of Elmet
    Ted Hughes and *Elmet* FAY GODWIN 106
    Yorkshire and *Elmet* ANTHONY THWAITE 109

What is the Truth?
    A Measure of Grace: The Teacher's Story JILL PIRRIE 112
    Portrait of Ted Hughes R. J. LLOYD 117

Shakespeare and the Goddess of Complete Being
    In the Company of Shakespeare and Ted Hughes
        DONYA FEUER 118

Winter Pollen
    Ted Hughes's 'Sylvia Plath: The Evolution of "Sheep in Fog"' –
    The Onlie Begetter ROY DAVIDS 122

Tales From Ovid
    Two Poets Laureate Joined by 2,000
        Years MELVYN BRAGG 124

Hoopoe MARINA WARNER 127

A Choice of Coleridge's Verse
Ted Hughes and Coleridge KATHLEEN RAINE 134

Birthday Letters
With Sorrow Doubled JON STALLWORTHY 138
Ted Hughes: *Birthday Letters* JOHN FOWLES 145
'Your roundy face' TOM PAULIN 147
Portrait of Ted Hughes by Sylvia Plath 151
'Daffodils' CLAIRE TOMALIN 152

Ted Hughes and Theatre
PETER BROOK 154
SIR JOHN GIELGUD 155
IRENE WORTH 156
The Death of Hippolytus LAVINIA GREENLAW 159
TIM SUPPLE 163

Uncollected
'Remembering Teheran' MICHAEL HOFMANN 167
'To Be Harry' RUTH FAINLIGHT 175
Manuscript of poem by Ted Hughes for Harry Fainlight 177

PART TWO: Poems for Ted Hughes

In a Junior School CHARLES CAUSLEY 181
The Fisherman GILLIAN CLARKE 183
Memories, Reflections, Gratitudes ROY DAVIDS 184
Shannon's Recovery MEDBH MCGUCKIAN 189
Planh for the Death of Ted Hughes W. S. MERWIN 190
Nine Ways of Looking at Ted Hughes
    ADRIAN MITCHELL 192
Herm PAUL MULDOON 196
A Deployment of Fashion LES MURRAY 197
Goa WILLIAM SCAMMELL 200
For T.H. CHARLES TOMLINSON 203

PART THREE: On Ted Hughes

Ted Hughes A. ALVAREZ 207
Ted Hughes's Poetry YEHUDA AMICHAI 212
With Ted Hughes BARRIE COOKE 214
Ted Hughes and South Yorkshire: 'A Motorbike'
    TERRY GIFFORD 216
Ted Hughes in Czech MIROSLAV HOLUB 219
Ted Hughes and the Calder Valley GLYN HUGHES 222
Ted Hughes: Children's Champion
    MICHAEL MORPURGO 225
Ted Hughes as Reader CHRISTOPHER REID 228
A Poet and a Critic KEITH SAGAR 230
Talisman PENELOPE SHUTTLE 255
Ted Hughes: A Short Memoir ALAN SILLITOE 259
Election '97 and Ted Hughes's Final Reading
    PETER STOTHARD 262
Ted Hughes on the Page STEPHEN TABOR 267

Select Book List 270
Notes on Contributors 272

Editor's Note

There was nothing fleeting or peripheral about Ted Hughes: his physical stature and the weight behind his words gave the impression of permanence. He was a fixed landmark from which to take bearings, the wisdom of ages reanimated in England. That fixity may help to explain the force of the shockwave that followed the news of his sudden death, and the profound sense of irreplaceable loss. The scale of that reaction illuminated the depth of respect for his extraordinary gifts as a writer: the unique force of his poetic imagination, his reverence for language, and his super-sensitive way of seeing and feeling.

I first discovered Ted Hughes's poetry in my school library in the early 1970s through the anthology *Six Modern Poets*. I remember the shock, and the feeling that this poet was revealing something crucial to me. I wrote to him shortly after that with some questions about his poetry, beginning a correspondence which was to endure for more than twenty years. His letters (the last one arrived just a few days before his death) were wonders, full of insights not just into his own writing but into the mystery of creative writing in general. He was sure of his poetic principles, and his thoughts were always fresh and invigorating. He was incapable of being dull and he was – above everything – his own man. Yet he was as much interested and intrigued by other people's writing as his own. I have vivid memories of an evening with Ted and his wife Carol at a performance of his new adaptation of Lorca's *Blood Wedding* at the Young Vic. The poetry was electric and the audience spellbound, yet Ted and Carol spoke not about the play, but asked me a series of questions about a small book which I had just produced. It was characteristic of them and very humbling.

Over the years I came to realize that many others shared this sense of Ted Hughes's qualities. At the time of his death I was compiling a book designed to capture this joint feeling. I had invited writers, and others who had known or worked with him, to choose a poem or book of his and describe why they valued it. Unaware of the seriousness of his illness, my idea was that the book should be ready in time for Hughes's seventieth birthday in 2000. The book would, I imagined, serve a double purpose: a birthday gift and an invigorating new route into the broad span of his work for readers who perhaps only knew him through the well-known anthology pieces. When I first floated the idea with him I wondered how he would react; he never chased praise nor measured the value of his work by the public reaction. However, he did feel (as I had discovered in those letters) considerable gratitude to those who read him closely, and he was always heartened when readers responded to the charge in his poetry. In the event, he gave my project his support with characteristic wry humour: 'I've always had in mind the Japanese proverb: "Applause is the beginning of abuse." But sometimes you feel you've run up a bit of credit.'

Just how much credit he had accrued quickly became clear from the enthusiastic and positive response from those I invited to take part, and the vibrancy of what they wrote. They had come to know Ted Hughes in many different ways – through poetry, through his work in theatre, through one of his many interests away from literature, and simply through friendship. The broad reach of their responses illuminates the breathtaking range of his writing and interests. It covers the full scope of his work, from early pieces to that extraordinary final collection, *Birthday Letters*. This is by any measure a towering and mesmeric body of writing, both for adults and for children. It has a ferocious driven intensity: what Thom Gunn once described as Hughes's 'concentrated energy'.

At the time of his death, many of the essays for this book had been finished, and more were near completion. Ted had seen a number of these and was deeply moved. They were, as they were meant to be, intensely personal responses to his work, full of incisive insight and enjoyment. Many contributors stuck closely to the brief of choosing a favourite poem or book, others ranged more widely, and some chose to write a new poem for him – about him. There was an overwhelming feeling among them that, although the book could no longer be the birthday gift for which it was intended, it should go ahead with its complimentary purpose: a celebration of Ted Hughes's achievement. Most decided to let their original piece stand. Others modified a little to reflect the impact of his loss.

The result is a vivid account of Ted Hughes and his work. The pieces here – both poetry and prose – give us new insights into the qualities of his life and writing. They pinpoint his openness to experience – no matter how painful – in striving for truth and integrity; his determination to understand the pulse at the heart of nature – in both its beauty and horror. The essays here celebrate, through their own openness and honesty, his unique capacity for conjuring that pulse.

As far as possible I have arranged the pieces in this book to move chronologically through Ted Hughes's work, culminating with some broader ranging essays and new poems. This arrangement illustrates both the diversity of his creations and his recurrent themes.

There can be little doubt that Ted Hughes will continue to be read with fascination, awe and enjoyment. The writers here show, through the closeness of their reading, some of the reasons why we can be so sure.

I am grateful to all those who have contributed to this book, and to my wife and children for their help and encouragement.

Nick Gammage

PART ONE

On the Poetry and Prose of Ted Hughes

KARL MILLER

Poetry from Cambridge 1952–54

In thinking about Ted Hughes and his poetry, I have often thought of the company he kept when he was young: of the poets, that is to say, who were his mates when he was a student at Cambridge. Ted stood out, as did Thom Gunn. But they were not the only good poets on the scene. Some of these, such as Peter Redgrove, went on to prominence as professional writers. Others did not. Several of them appeared in an anthology I edited, *Poetry from Cambridge 1952–54*.

I don't think I realized at the time what a rich scene this was. But it was certainly apparent that to a number of the young men and women who had gathered in the town from all points of the compass, poetry was a pleasure. It was not beyond them. It was not a dead art. They wanted to get on with it. One of those who did well with it, in my opinion, was the late Geoffrey Strickland, who has in the anthology a short, somewhat Ronsardian poem in which old age is foresuffered, or foresavoured, in a jealous trance. This 'Poem in April' seems even better to me now than it did then.

Like an old pensioner, the entire day
I have sat here in the window bay
Absorbed almost contentedly
With what you will have worn for him,
What you will say,

[3]

Over which hills and through which woods
You will have walked and how your throat
Will have been raised to his embrace.
My attentive mind has run before
With its queer knowledge of woods,
Its old man's passion indulging your
Passion as if in this it were to gloat
On its own hardening and decay.

I don't suggest that Ted Hughes owed his start as a poet to participation in a school of poets. But I do suggest that it may have been a help to him to discover that there was a common pursuit of poetry, as well as of criticism, in 1950s Cambridge. For all the talk there had been of the decline of the art, it seemed natural to some twenty people, met together in this particular, partly unpropitious, self-consciously critical place, to have a shot at writing verse. Few of them were put off, I should add, and some of them were turned on, as poets, by F. R. Leavis's severities of the time; his call for a 'common pursuit of true judgement' was rarely seen as a threat. Not that he was likely to have read their works, with the possible exception of those of his pupil, Strickland, whose 'Poem in April' has Leavis in it, as well as Ronsard. Metrically and otherwise, it is the sort of poem this critic liked to discuss. I can just picture him expounding the enjambement that occurs in the course of the last three lines, with their important equal stress on 'your' and ' Passion'.

The three poems by Ted which appeared in the anthology are markedly different from Geoffrey Strickland's and from one another. They are youthful pieces, two of which may from an early stage have been classed by the writer as juvenilia. But the roughness and innocence they show belong to an intent; they are not there in default of something better, more 'mature'. There is no lack of skill that I can see. The youthfulness of the three poems consists of the freshness and vigour of their spread wings, of the first full flights they may possibly have represented. 'The Little Boys and the Seasons' is influenced by the youthful Blake of the *Poetical Sketches* and by the Dylan Thomas of 'Fern Hill' ('merry as apples'). But it's very much its own poem. There's nothing quite like it even in the subsequent Hughes's oeuvre. The long loose lines have a vernacular quality, as of schoolboy slang made extraordinarily eloquent, as of the schoolboy whom Ted can only recently have grown old enough to be able to recollect, to look back on. Verse one, with its Primavera, reads:

> One came out of the wood. 'What a bit of a girl,'
> The small boys cried, 'To make my elder brother daft,   .
> Tossing her petticoats under the bushes. O we know,
> We know all about you: there's a story.
> Well we don't want your tinny birds with their noise,
> And we don't want your soppy flowers with their smells,
> And you can just take all that make-up off our garden,
> And stop giving the animals ideas with your eyes.'
> And she cried a cloud and all the children ran in.

And so on through the seasons to the emergence, from the sea, of winter, the hard captain,

>   stamping
> Up and down the fields with the nails in his boots.

The second poem is among the earliest of Hughes's bird and beast poems, those poems in which animals give him ideas with their eyes. Here is his celebrated jaguar, watched in awe through the bars of a cage in a zoo, burning bright, 'the crazed eye satisfied to be blind in fire' while 'the apes yawn and adore their fleas in the sun'.

The third poem is a poem by the future Poet Laureate about artist and audience, artist and patron: 'The Court-Tumbler and Satirist'. Princes are heard here proclaiming the role of the 'true artist' as that of a rutter, a scrambler after girls, and disdaining the court jester's, the tumbler's, role as that of a poor fish coaxing smiles from the grand ladies of the court. But then the poem goes on to say that the tumbler is tumbling these very ladies – in a manner not remote, one might think, from that in which, according to these princes, the true artist comports himself. 'Each starchy beauty,' the poem ends,

> Gets all that necessity can get from duty
> Under that enviable accomplished back.

The poem gives an account of the command performances to which artists may have to respond – whether by appointment to their majesties, or to the Millennium Dome, or as crowd-pleasers on television: an account of the hostility this can inspire on both sides of the footlights, and of a hidden power exercised by such performers. It is not, of course, a job description for the post of Poet Laureate, and can hardly have presaged any ructions or subversions at Buckingham Palace.

It is written in the Jacobean style which appealed at this point both to Ted Hughes and to Thom Gunn. Donne's words, with the 'masculine persuasive force' which he himself attributed to them, mattered to both writers, and Ben Jonson's words mattered also to Gunn. A directness, an outspokenness, a violent figurative energy, were the result. A senior Cambridge academic, an admirable man, was puzzled by the Hughes's poems in the anthology, and the odds were that young readers would take to them before their parents did. They were young poems, after all, and gifted poems too, expressive of an 'enviable accomplished back', a straight back and burning eye. None deserves to prowl behind the bars of a juvenilia.

ADAM THORPE

Ted Hughes and *The Hawk in the Rain*

My parents were in Africa and I was in England, at a boarding school in the depths of Wiltshire. I was fourteen, miserable and homesick. But where was home? In Douala, the great steamy port of Cameroon, dominated by its volcano and vast muddy estuary, fringed by mangrove swamps and monkey-chattering bush? Or in my childhood haunts among the Chiltern Hills – soft beechwoods and pasture and ordinary sleepy Chesham?

I was beginning to get interested in poetry, as something that was making me feel peculiar in a pleasant way. I decided to compile an anthology, for my sister, of poems to do with animals. At the time, I wanted to be a warden of a safari park. I reckoned that animals were nicer than humans – especially the human sub-species of public schoolboy. So I leafed through other general anthologies and picked out animal poems. That wonderful series called *Voices* came in useful. Maybe it was in one of their potpourris of poems and pictures that I happened across, pretty well simultaneously, D. H. Lawrence's 'Snake' and Ted Hughes's 'The Horses'. I remember now the electric feeling of pleasure as I set them down as neatly as I could with my fat fountain pen, cutting pictures out of magazines as illustration.

Lawrence's poem snaked down like its subject, I could see that. That was the clever trick of it. It seemed to go on forever, but I made no mistakes and blotted it with a sense of triumph. Then there was the poem by Ted Hughes. As I copied it down at my cubby-hole of a desk, surrounded by the raucous noise of pubescent hobbledehoys, I too climbed through the silent, pre-dawn woods, chill with frost. I too received the wisdom of the stone-like horses and felt the wonder and fear of the erupting dawn as it burned around them, thawing the world but not their patient hung heads. And then the last little section made me want to cry (but I didn't, of course – that was the law then):

In din of the crowded streets, going among the years, the faces,
May I still meet my memory in so lonely a place

Between the streams and the red clouds, hearing curlews,
Hearing the horizons endure.

Curlews were peewits, weren't they? I knew what peewits sounded like. On my solitary bike-rides or long walks over the Wiltshire downs, I'd keep hearing their plaintive mew. I saw the poet holding this little treasure of a memory like a fetish, making him strong. I saw that it didn't matter being lonely. Being lonely was a kind of strength. The din of the room became both more hateful and less overpowering, less invasive.

I blotted the poem and saw how the spaces between the stanzas looked even broader in my handwritten version. Those long stretched lines had been difficult to master, keeping them within the width of the page and reasonably straight. It was like galloping on a horse, which I had actually done once, by mistake. I tried to work out how Hughes had managed to make such extraordinary music without rhyme, as if he was talking to you. Talking in a deep, dramatic way but not in a way that sounded as if he was quoting from a poem. I failed to work it out. It was a sort of spell, the runes of which I had to learn by absorption. I had written poems myself, and found rhyme and metre quite easy in my simple way. This was more mysterious, like Shakespeare's blank verse or the ringing cadences of the old Bible in church services.

A couple of years later (judging by the date in my copy) I found *The Hawk in the Rain* in the school's second-hand books department. According to its stamp, it had been there since 1958 – returned a year after publication, and lying unclaimed for some sixteen years! Its price of five shillings had been decimalized, at least. It wasn't too dusty, either – until I took it home to Africa that holiday, when the harmattan was blowing its fine red sand everywhere. The book become a sort of fetish, bouncing about in the back of our rusty old Peugeot whenever we took off on the main road out of Douala. This main road was a dirt-track full of pot-holes and wrecked taxis, cut straight through the bush. I can see the book now, lying on the back shelf, rippling in the sultry heat, as a wall of endless coppery trees passed us on each side. The book's first line, 'I drown in the drumming ploughland', took me straight back to England, its cool wet muddiness, its grey-toned mire. But it had in it all the violence and fury of the African climate in the rainy season, drumming on the roofs like infinite troops of iron-shod cavalry, gouging out ravines in the road, using up all the air. One's face running with sweat at the window, feeling the odd cool billow of wind, bringing the giant smells of vegetation.

I'd repeat that first stanza like a charm. It was one of my homes, I suppose. The mud below, the hawk above, the rain in between. Sense and intellect, body and mind, flesh and spirit, persistence and inspiration, the particular and the universal, linked by the liquid drumming of the vital fire, metamorphosed into the clicks and glottals and sibilants and aspirates of our wonderful native tongue:

I drown in the drumming ploughland, I drag up
Heel after heel from the swallowing of the earth's mouth,
From clay that clutches my each step to the ankle
With the habit of the dogged grave, but the hawk

Effortlessly at height hangs his still eye.

Later, when Douala had been left behind, I was offered the chance to have a book of my choice bound there in gold-tooled calfskin, the way it used to be done. I chose my first-edition paperback of

Moortown. The unknown binder in some Douala backstreet has whorled the endpapers with muddy ochre and tooled a beautiful gold tree on the hard, thick spine with its leathern ribs. Never mind that the cheapskate paper has yellowed: the book is a symbol of Africa and England whorled together in my head, its animist force taking me back to the sacred bull I once saw in the remote northern part of Cameroon, pacing enormous in its wooden cage, the cage set into the chief's rambling earth palace. When I think of Hughes's poetry, I think of that sacred bull. There it stared at us out of its darkness: a precious thing, full of strange power. A vessel of pungent mystery.

LINDSAY CLARKE

'Wind'

===

This house has been far out at sea all night,
The woods crashing through darkness, the booming hills,
Winds stampeding the fields under the window
Floundering black astride and blinding wet

Till day rose; then under an orange sky
the hills had new places, and wind wielded
Blade-light, luminous black and emerald,
Flexing like the lens of a mad eye.

At noon I scaled along the house-side as far as
The coal-house door. Once I looked up –
Through the brunt wind that dented the balls of my eyes
The tent of the hills drummed and strained its guyrope,

The fields quivering, the skyline a grimace,
At any second to bang and vanish with a flap:
The wind flung a magpie away and a black–
Back gull bent like an iron bar slowly. The house

Rang like some fine green goblet in the note
That any second would shatter it. Now deep
In chairs, in front of the great fire, we grip
Our hearts, and cannot entertain book, thought

Or each other. We watch the fire blazing,
And feel the roots of the house move, but sit on,
Seeing the windows tremble to come in,
Hearing the stones cry out under the horizons.

Sometimes, in a culture bereft of other meaningful rites of passage, a book encountered at the right moment can act on the imagination with the force of an initiatory ordeal. Certainly something of the sort felt true for me when I was a moody, sixth form A level student at Heath Grammar School in Halifax, a little over forty years ago.

My weekly timetable of English, History and Art left plenty of gaps for private study, and I spent a lot of time mooching about in the school library. Its windows looked out to where Beacon Hill loomed over the town with its restless-making reminder that, beyond the valley's blackened congregation of mills and factories and spires, wilder horizons were unfolding across a raw landscape of high moorland and introverted crags, of ling and blowing cotton-grass, of water, rock, and wind.

Meanwhile, inside the library a desultory collection of books lolled in their cases. Most of them were heirlooms from the time when the Elizabethan Free School was rebuilt in 1878, but a few, more recent acquisitions were of particular interest to me. Among them were Yeats's edition of the *Oxford Book of Modern Verse* and a black-bound volume of T. S. Eliot's *Collected Poems*, for around that time I'd begun to fancy myself a poet.

Enthused by the delusion, and for shamelessly selfish reasons, I put pressure on our English teacher, 'Biddy', to respond to a leaflet from the Poetry Book Society which offered what sounded to me like a good deal. In return for a modest annual subscription, the library's stock would be enlivened by the work of two contemporary poets each year. Eventually Biddy agreed that it wouldn't wreck his Department's budget for 1957 if we gave the thing a try.

I got to unpack the first book when it came. I had turned only a few pages when a big wind came blowing out at me. It bustled me back on my heels, picked me up, tossed me about for a time, then blew me clear away. Watching all the known world pitch and roll beneath me, I was gone from the library, up across the mucky town, down the cleft of the Calder Valley and out towards Mytholmroyd where the voice of this breathtaking wind had first blown from.

Its accent was recognizably local. I heard it gusting in vowels flat as the rainwater in a moorland reservoir. Its tongue clattered out a palate-dance of consonants that strummed with Pennine energy. For this was a local gale, straight off Top Withens, blowing the whole West Riding into shape, then out of it again, snatching up ships and horses, tents and iron bars in its frenzy, yet trembling with a nervous kind of awe at all it stumbled on. I stood in the silence of the school library, blinking in the teeth of the gale, and knew that poetry was alive, immediate, and *here*.

As Ted Hughes wrote later: 'Almost every poet when he mentions the wind, touches one of his good moments of poetry.' The young contender behind *The Hawk in the Rain* knew who set the standards, and he was truly on his mettle in this poem. In retrospect one wonders whether he also sensed its oracular air of prophecy, that a whole life might have to be lived in the hard eye of that wind?

I came to realize much later this extraordinary man from Mytholmroyd was also crossing the weird, metamorphic land-scape of the alchemical imagination far ahead of me. It gave a strange kind of comfort, at once heartening and gruelling, to watch him pass through the bleak nigredo of *Crow*, across grim *Elmet,* down among the *Cave Birds*, and on to the creatures of light in the radiance of *River*'s end. Sadly, that lifetime's journey has ended now, but the commitment to its rigours that took him ever further into the interpenetrating realms of myth and memory has proved so deep-searching that the perspectives he opened on the poetics of the soul will continue to unfold as long as there are readers.

When I look back at 'Wind' now it makes me think of the robust emblem in Michael Maier's *Atalanta Fugiens* where a vortex of wind whirls from the head of a naked man to spin the Philosopher's Stone from air. But I knew nothing of such hermetic images in 1957. Nor could I have guessed then how widely Ted Hughes's important essay on 'Myth and Education' would later enlarge my understanding, both as teacher and writer, of the mediating role of the imagination – though a whole novel would one day shape itself round what he showed me there of its capacity to negotiate between the inner and the outer worlds. No, all that mattered to me at seventeen when I first read 'Wind' was that I shared my natal landscape with a prodigious new poet who had proved that poetry was still able to breath visionary fire.

I took this poem personally. It filled me with a quickening sense of exhilaration and dread. In its appetite for language, its generation and consumption of metaphor, its attention to colour, form, scale and stress, and the ardour with which its power of hyperbolic invention stilled itself at last to a steady, unflinching gaze, it seemed to demonstrate exactly why writing mattered.

Like the people in the poem, I felt the wind had gripped my heart. It began to answer passionate questions that I hardly dared to put, while posing others that I wasn't ready yet to answer. In doing so, it joined the converging forces that were blowing me through to a risky place where, in the long run at least, no other life than a writer's life would do.

With the rough affection of the elder brother that I never had and always wanted, it stretched and dared and bullied me. For a book, as I say, can offer a kind of initiation. It may not even take a whole book: at the right time just a single, hard-earned poem will serve; and I think this poem astonished me to consciousness.

ALAN GOULD

Lupercal

═══

I have always found *Lupercal* a dazzling collection, containing
what are, in my view, among the finest evocations of feral and
country life in the English language. As with Ted Hughes's first
book, *The Hawk in the Rain*, the diction in these poems has a
feeling-one's-way ductility, Shakespearian in cadence, as is the
metaphysical manner in which perceptions are juxtaposed. Here
is the otter from the poem of that title:

> The heart beats thick,
> Big trout muscle out of the dead cold;
> Blood is the belly of logic; he will lick
> The fishbone bare. And can take stolen hold
>
> On a bitch otter in a field full
> Of nervous horses, but linger nowhere.
> Yanked above hounds, reverts to nothing at all,
> To this long pelt over the back of a chair.

In poems like this one, or 'Hawk Roosting', 'Pike', 'View of a
Pig', 'November' and many others, it is the *rapture* inherent in
the poet's voice that I would most like to identify. For what I find
so arresting about the poet's voice here is the intentness of the
observing eye that these words seem to disclose. The imaging
and the verbal parts of the mind could not be in a more finely
tuned co-ordination with each other and the syntax has the

pressure of one lost in the exhilaration of an interest. Furthermore, here is rapture which, without the least contriving, is sacral. These poems carry such a charge of sympathy for the strangeness of the world of the creatures that the poet becomes our mediator with a dimension of animistic mystery. What distinguishes these poems as spiritual exploration rather than occasional pastoral descriptions is the delicacy, the *tenderness*, with which details touch and unfold the essentials of Creation. For instance, the stoical trust of the tramp in 'November' which so disconcerts the speaker identifies also a principle of creaturely trust. The self-possession of the hawk as it solemnly declares its hawkhood in 'Hawk Roosting' is a principle of creaturely self-possession. The blunt deadness of the pig in 'View of a Pig' is a principle of lifelessness stripped of funereal adornments. Thus the poems of *Lupercal* create, not only a gallery of creatures, but the world of creatures and the essential traits that govern that world's existence.

To be moved, as a human reader, by these essentials is to enter a dimension, strange while being also disconcertingly close to our own familiar world of social interdependence and culture, and one from which withdrawal is difficult. The difficulty lies, I suspect, in reasons very similar to those which made it so hard for Gulliver to re-adjust to human society after his sojourn with the Houyhnhnms in the fourth book of his travels. Gulliver experiences a world governed by the rational virtues; Hughes observes a world where no aspect of being can be suppressed. Both throw into high relief the deluded, suppressive, and ineffectual parts of human existence, prompting not so much contempt for it, as a simple loss of interest in the human domain. By no means does Hughes forget this domain. He simply shifts it from the centre of Creation. He looks outside man for the clues to psychic health in man. Herein lies the spiritual risk he undertakes in his poems, for behind these figurative animal portraits there have been invoked the incalculable powers of amoral existence with their alluring promise of psychic health. In *Wodwo* and *Crow*, the two books that followed *Lupercal*, these powers confront and test more urgently the behaviour of men and man's gods and god-substitutes.

(This is taken from a longer essay on Ted Hughes's work, entitled 'Ted Hughes and Self Possession'.)

JAMES LASDUN

Notes on a Footnote

The pig lay on a barrow dead.
It weighed, they said, as much as three men.
Its eyes closed, pink white eyelashes.
Its trotters stuck straight out.

Such weight and thick pink bulk
Set in death seemed not just dead.
It was less than lifeless, further off,
It was like a sack of wheat.

I thumped it without feeling remorse.
One feels guilty insulting the dead,
Walking on graves. But this pig
Did not seem able to accuse.

It was too dead. Just so much
A poundage of lard and pork.
Its last dignity had entirely gone.
It was not a figure of fun.

Too dead now to pity.
To remember its life, din, stronghold
Of earthly pleasure as it had been,
Seemed a false effort, and off the point.

Too deadly factual. Its weight
Oppressed me – how could it be moved?
And the trouble of cutting it up!
The gash in its throat was shocking, but not pathetic.

Once I ran at a fair in the noise
To catch a greased piglet
That was faster and nimbler than a cat,
Its squeal was the rending of metal.

Pigs must have hot blood, they feel like ovens.
Their bite is worse than a horse's –
They chop a half-moon clean out.
They eat cinders, dead cats.

Distinctions and admirations such
As this one was long finished with.
I stared at it a long time. They were going to scald it,
Scald it and scour it like a doorstep.

I first read 'View of a Pig' at school. I was fifteen or so and not much interested in poetry, but this poem had a distinct and lingering effect on me. It left me feeling oddly oppressed, as though I were being crushed under a dead weight – of the dead pig itself, I suppose. Reading it again now I see that this was probably the feeling Hughes himself was intending to communicate. Unlike most of his animal portraits, which attempt in words what the living energies of nature contrive in nerve, muscle and bone, this one seems motivated by a vision of a kind of active inertia. The dead pig, 'a sack of wheat', 'a doorstep', is glimpsed in a condition of lifelessness that stands in the same relation to mere death as a black hole does to a dead planet. It positively drains life from the space around it, leaving speaker and reader exhausted, depleted, depressed: 'it was less than lifeless, further off'.

Like the image of Saturn in Keats's 'Hyperion' – his right hand 'nerveless, listless and dead' – such deathly visions (which tend to be granted mainly to poets with a peculiar responsiveness to the vibrancy of living things) are perhaps best understood as versions of their own opposite – vitality temporarily held in a kind of allotropic freeze. The view of this pig is suffused with an immense, thwarted desire to locate the secret energies of the animal. Something vast is apprehended but it lies just off the page, one stray particle of it drifting over in the form of the greased piglet remembered from a fair – 'faster and nimbler than a cat' – but the bulk of it bafflingly occluded.

It should surprise no one that something so powerfully latent should finally erupt. Saturn's hand comes electrifyingly to life in the opening lines of the famous fragment to Fanny Brawne – 'This living hand, now warm and capable / Of earnest grasping' . . . In Hughes the repolarizing process is longer and more elaborate. It comes by way of what increasingly appears to have been one of the most far-reaching sustained meditations ever undertaken by an English poet on the nature of poetic creation, principally in Shakespeare, but also – by various means – in Ovid, Coleridge and Sylvia Plath. It is both figuratively and literally a footnote to these meditations, but it is surely one of the great footnotes in the language.

Anyone who has had the pleasure of reading Hughes's magisterial *Shakespeare and the Goddess of Complete Being* will remember its exhilarating pursuit of the seminal (in every sense) image of the wild boar from Ovid's 'Venus and Adonis', as it plunges from the relative domesticity of Ovid's mind into the surging wilds of Shakespeare's, and proceeds to rampage its way through his entire opus. Bearing in mind that deader-than-dead pig on its barrow, this mythical counterpart, with its privileged mobility between this world and the underworld, surely promises to tell us something about Ted Hughes as well as Shakespeare.

The footnote, which is a poem in all but name (it even looks like one in its narrow columns), comes on page 11 of my edition. It glosses an item in a list of motifs that Shakespeare appropriates from Venus and Adonis, to wit: 'The Boar is also the Goddess of the Underworld'. As if startled by his own suggestion of unstable gender in this most masculine of creatures, and anxious to dampen any frisson this might arouse, Hughes embarks on a footnote that at first appears to be wearily academic: 'The Boar's peculiarly hermaphroditic nature is almost universally recognized in mythology . . .' However, the poet soon gets the better of the anthropologist, and what follows might be entitled (along the lines of the two Jaguar poems) 'Second View of a Pig'. The pig in the first poem was emphatically neuter, an 'it'. As with Keats, the apposition of the feminine (the thought of Fanny Brawne) to the formerly enervated subject, seems to shock it into sudden vivid life. The pig that takes over this anecdote has a definite gender. She is a sow; the mother of all sows you might say, and she unleashes an imaginative *tour de force* on the subject of 'the elemental mother' that combines the antic grotesquerie of the Wife of Bath, with the wry daemonism of Plath's Lady Lazarus or her bee queen from 'Stings'. Here she is, in her original columnar form:

> Her combi-
> nation of gross whiskery nakedness and
> riotous carnality is seized by the mythic
> imagination, evidently, as a sort of uterus on
> the loose – upholstered with breasts, not so
> much many-breasted as a mobile tub entirely
> made of female sexual parts, a woman-sized,
> multiple udder on trotters. Most alarming of
> all is that elephantine, lolling mouth under
> her great ear-flaps, like a Brueghelesque
> nightmare vagina, baggy with over-
> production, famous for gobbling her piglets,
> magnified and shameless, exuberantly omni-
> vorous and insatiable, swamping the senses . . .
> . . . she fulfils an ambiguous lunar
> role. Her variable dark part is sinister, not
> only because she incorporates more shock-
> ing physical familiarity, more radical enter-
> prise, more rapturous appetite, cruder

travesties of infantile memory, wilder
nostalgias, than the cow, but because she is
inseparable from the lethal factor of the
Boar, who carries the same vaginal grin yet
is prodigiously virile –

The 'hermaphroditic' note relates of course to the second key
story from Ovid, 'Hermaphroditus', which Shakespeare combined with Ovid's 'Venus and Adonis' to form his own version of
the latter. Both of the Ovidian sources were among the four tales
Ted Hughes translated so superbly for the anthology *After Ovid*:
New Metamorphoses which I edited with Michael Hofmann.
The immersion in Shakespeare and Ovid, not to mention
Hughes's investigation of the shape-shifting phantasms of
Coleridge's imagination, lend to the resurrection of this humble
farmyard creature a depth of human meaning and mythopoeic
resonance it might not have acquired thirty-odd years ago, when
its death was first reported. So too, though one hesitates to
intrude here, does Hughes's own evolving position in a
contemporary literary myth in which archetypes of the Male
and the Female, the Living and the Dead are so potently and
complexly brought together. With the immense erudition and
analytic powers he commanded at the time of his death, the
verbal expressiveness as supple and minutely accurate as ever,
and the recent admittance of deeply personal material to the
published work, one can only wonder what further miracles of
transformation await discovery in this splendid late flowering of
an exemplary career.

BLAKE MORRISON

Wodwo

Ted Hughes's collection *Wodwo* came out in 1967, when I was sixteen. It was his third collection, published ten years after *The Hawk in the Rain* and seven after *Lupercal.* I wish I could say I read it at the time but I had other things on my mind. Though poetry was among those things, the poets I was taught at school – Robert Browning, Thomas Hardy, Wilfred Owen, Siegfried Sassoon, T. S. Eliot, W. H. Auden – went up only to 1939, and those I was discovering outside school – the Liverpool poets, the Barrow poets, Adrian Mitchell – were popular (and pop-influenced) performers.

It's a pity I didn't come across Hughes's work then. Without him I got the idea that poetry happened in other times or, if in my own time, in other, more swingingly urban places. With him, I'd have seen that it could happen in my own valleys and hills. Though by this point he had moved south, the Pennine contours of his work are unmistakeable. Sodden fells, 'old hairy moors', sheep-cropped summits, hills 'hoisting heather and stones to the sky', the tear of a curlew, an outcrop of rock 'hoarding its nothings', winds stampeding the fields, the tent of the hills drumming and straining its guyrope, magpies flung away in the wind, a black-back gull bending like an iron bar slowly, skylarks going up 'like a warning', 'mist-gulfs of no-thinking,' 'the summer turf's heat-rise', gnats dancing at evening, the stones crying out under the horizon: this was my home ground, and no matter how darkly distinctive Hughes's interpretation I'd have recognized it at once. Heptonstall was only twenty miles off, and to anyone living thereabouts Hughes's ode to its black persistence wouldn't have seemed Beckettian, or existentialist, or post-holocaust, but simply accurate topographical transcription:

> Life tries.
> Death tries.
> The stone tries.
> Only the rain never tires.

It's easy to imagine the last line having been prompted by a typo: transpose two letters and the effort of 'tries' becomes the surrender of 'tires', an accident which Hughes uses to happy effect. It's not that he's being playful, exactly, but jokes about the rain never letting up are standard in the Pennines, and it's important to hear that note of gruff comedy. Hughes can sound nihilistic but he isn't. Even in 'Pibroch', which resonates with the word 'nothing' and accompanyingly glum adjectives – 'meaningless', 'without purpose', 'bored' – there's a strange lift and lightness at the end, rather like the experience of seeing stars after getting a knock to the head:

> Minute after minute, aeon after aeon,
> Nothing lets up or develops.
> And this is neither a bad variant nor a tryout.
> This is where the staring angels go through.
> This is where all the stars bow down.

It's often said, disparagingly, that Hughes can't do people. But he does, with great authority, the trials people have to face – including the threat of death, and the threat of being bored to death. If people don't loom as large as they might in his work, a certain under-populatedness is apt for evoking the area where he grew up, which had been more populous once, before the mills closed and the jobs went.

If I'd read Hughes at sixteen I might not have felt an aspiring writer had to move away from Yorkshire in order to work. As it was, I didn't come across him until I was living in London in my early twenties, at the back end of 1973, by which point I saw him through the eyes of A. Alvarez. I read *The Savage God*, Alvarez's study of art and suicide. I read *The New Poetry*, Alvarez's anthology, and his accompanying essay on behalf of the 'extremist' tendency in modern poetry. I read Sylvia Plath. I read *Crow*, which had come out the previous year. Only then did I read Hughes's earlier work. By that point it was too late. In thrall to Alvarez, and his thesis of romantic risk and agony, I saw Hughes as a misanthrope whose sense of life as stony waste and animal horror had been compounded by the suicide of his wife. The humour, stoicism, loving detail – these I hardly saw at all.

Wildly though I misread it, *Wodwo* made a deep impression, and it still seems to me that it's the book in which Hughes found his mature voice. *The Hawk in the Rain* has three terrific poems – 'The Thought-Fox', 'Wind' and 'October Dawn' – but much of the collection is awkwardly caught between the fever of late Yeats (that is, the Yeats of the Crazy Jane poems) and an impulse to write rational, well-made Movement verse (throughout the moving 'Six Young Men', for example, one of several poems preoccupied with the First World War, there's the rumble of Larkin's 'Church Going'). *Lupercal* has a higher strike-rate – 'Pike', 'Thrushes', 'Hawk Roosting', 'View of a Pig', 'The Bull Moses', 'Snowdrop' – but in many of its poems Hughes is still inhibited by the musical logic of the quatrain. Both books contain items best forgotten, not so much because of machismo and misogyny (see 'Secretary' for example – or rather, don't) but because of their borrowed attitudes and borrowed styles. It's not surprising or especially lamentable: both collections were written before Hughes was thirty, when most British poets are still struggling to amass half a collection worth putting in for an Eric Gregory award. But compared to *Moortown*, say, the first two books are more about promise than achievement.

By contrast *Wodwo* came out when Hughes was thirty-seven, by which time a lot had happened to him, in art as well as life. It's a baggy book, with a middle section containing five stories and a play, a structure which may owe something to Robert Lowell's *Life Studies*. Hughes has none of Lowell's confessional instincts. But in its own way, through part-imaginary landscapes and creatures, *Wodwo* does become autobiography.

Forced to keep just one *Wodwo* poem to take to a desert island, in the face of enormous competition from 'Thistles', 'Still Life', 'Skylarks', 'Gnat-Psalm' and 'Full Moon and Little Frieda', it was the title-poem I'd have chosen then. Twenty-five years later, it still is.

> What am I? Nosing here, turning leaves over
> Following a faint stain on the air to the river's edge
> I enter water. What am I to split
> the glassy grain of water looking upward I see the bed
> Of the river above me upside down very clear . . .

Hughes found the word 'wodwo' in *Sir Gawain and the Green Knight* ('Sumwhyle with wormez he werrez, and with wolues als / Sumwhyle with wodwos, that woned in the knarrez'), where it's glossed as 'troll' or 'satyr'. Apart from 'etaynes' (giants or ogres), the other enemies Gawain is mentioned as battling with at that point are animal: wolves, bears, boars, bulls and dragons. Hughes seems to have taken his hint from this: we don't know what the wodwo is, and nor does the wodwo, but its nosing and rooting suggest an animal (otter, beaver, anteater) more than they do a human form. What may be human in the wodwo is its intelligence and self-consciousness – its wanting to understand why it does what it does even while doing it. If it is human, it can only be early human – Neanderthal, perhaps, or in some way 'savage'. Comparisons might be made with William Golding's *The Inheritors* (1955), which is about Neanderthal man at the point of being usurped by *Homo sapiens*:

> The stick began to grow shorter at both ends. Then it shot out to full length again.
> The dead tree by Lok's ear acquired a voice.
> 'Clop!'

His ears twitched and he turned to the tree. By his face there had grown a twig: a twig that smelt of other, and of goose, and of the bitter berries that Lok's stomach told him he must not eat. This twig had a white bone at the end. There were hooks in the bone and sticky brown stuff hung in the crooks.

This passage from *The Inheritors* describes the shooting of a poisoned arrow from a bow. Lok, the innocent Neanderthal, doesn't realize this, or can't put it into words, but we, as readers, led on by hints from Golding, can and do. Therein lies an important difference to 'Wodwo', which can't be unpicked like a crossword puzzle: the nature of the beast remains a mystery, to Hughes as well as to us:

> What am I doing here in mid-air? Why do I find
> this frog so interesting as I inspect its most secret
> interior and make it my own? Do these weeds
> know me and name me to each other have they
> seen me before, do I fit in their world? I seem
> separate from the ground and not rooted but dropped
> out of nothing casually I've no threads
> fastening me to anything I can go anywhere
> I seem to have been given the freedom
> of this place . . .

Hughes himself seems to have discovered a new freedom here which is partly stylistic: minimal punctuation, enjambement, lower-case line beginnings, a loose blank verse. The syntactical ambiguities as to where one sentence ends and another begins are highly appropriate, expressing as they do the wodwo's confusion about where *it* (or he or she) begins and ends:

> And picking
> bits of bark off this rotten stump gives me
> no pleasure and it's no use so why do I do it
> me and doing that have coincided very queerly
> But what shall I be called am I the first
> have I an owner what shape am I what

[27]

shape am I am I huge if I go
to the end on this way past these trees and past these
    trees

Whether hawks roosting or pike stunned by their own grandeur, the creatures in Hughes's first two books are violent, imperious, in control. *Wodwo* marks a turning point: something humble and chastened arrives; tentative questions replace confident end-stops; instead of assertions of authority we get confessions of ignorance. Those looking for easy autobiographical readings of Hughes tend to bypass *Wodwo* and leap to *Crow*, finding in its cartoon violence and blackness an expression of life in turmoil after Sylvia Plath's death. But in the title poem of *Wodwo* is a more subtly personal subtext. The young Hughes's insights into the dark side of nature, in his first two collections, can be thrilling but also easy and callow: he has looked, and seen, and pretends to have the key. The Hughes of *Wodwo*, having lived a bit in the darkness, has lost his youthful swagger: he has looked, and seen, but is no longer sure how to describe what he has found. Far from knowing all the answers, he now treats poetry as a form of quest:

for the moment if I sit still how everything
stops to watch me I suppose I am the exact centre
but there's all this what is it roots
roots roots roots and here's the water
again very queer but I'll go on looking

'I'll go on looking' means: To be continued. There is no full stop. It also implies a curiosity and perseverance, which we meet again in the irrepressible crow of *Crow*. However hard the knocks, however yawning the chasms, the hero never abandons his quest. You don't give up. You go on looking. It's the tale of a wodwo. But it's also the story of Ted Hughes.

Postscript

I wrote the above piece a couple of months before Ted Hughes's death, in the expectation that, like his wodwo, he'd be able to 'go on looking' for some time yet. I knew he was ill, and had even heard the word 'cancer' mentioned, which helped explain the urgency behind the publication of *Birthday Letters*. But the possibility of him not living to see his seventieth birthday didn't occur. I was in North America when news of his death broke, and felt stunned and very isolated, unable to explain to anyone there what a loss British poetry had just suffered – as if a giant oak had toppled, leaving only saplings below. In that continent, poets and critics either demonize Hughes or regard him as a minor adjunct to Sylvia Plath. They don't seem aware of the range and power of his achievement. He wasn't given his due in Britain, either, but from the mid-1990s a feeling grew that he'd suffered and been baited long enough. The acclaim for *Tales from Ovid* and the *Birthday Letters* was some kind of reparation. He said he didn't read reviews, but I hope he sensed the warmth of the public's response in his last months.

Ted was a shy man, fearful of the intrusions of both camera and telephone. Even if the circumstances of his life had been different, he'd not have been one for television interviews and self-promotional tours. As it was, heckled and harassed by adherents of what he called the Plath Fantasia, he had to retreat even further than his nature prompted, at the risk of being thought haughty and cold. In reality, he was far from either. Friends would often feel the heat of his latest enthusiasm, whether for Coleridge or memory-training or new methods of preserving threatened species. In his fervour, he could sound a bit batty: you sat by the fire of his discourses, unsure what to make of them or how to respond. But he was gentle, and generous, and – though not one for jokes – he had a rich laugh.

I got to know him through judging children's poetry competitions together and once took my own children to his home, where they were invited to dress up in various animal skins which Ted rushed to bring from adjoining rooms (Carol, his wife, took photos, but something was wrong with the camera and – typically Hughesian, somehow – the shots didn't turn out). 'I hope they didn't become fur-fetishists after that morning', Ted wrote in his last card to me. My children will always remember his eager kindness that morning. It's in his writing, though, that he would want to be remembered – where the man still lives. His poetry is not overtly self-expressing. But it tells the stories that most mattered to him. And it's where we know him best.

'Full Moon and Little Frieda'

A cool small evening shrunk to a dog bark and the
   clank of a bucket –

And you listening.
A spider's web, tense for the dew's touch.
A pail lifted, still and brimming – mirror
To tempt a first star to a tremor.

Cows are going home in the lane there, looping the
   hedges with their warm wreaths of breath –
A dark river of blood, many boulders
Balancing unspilled milk.

'Moon!' you cry suddenly, 'Moon! Moon!'

The moon has stepped back like an artist gazing
   amazed at a work

That points at him amazed.

It was 1967 or 1968, and I was fifteen or sixteen, and there was
an LP with an almost all-white sleeve. It had the poets' names
along the bottom edge: Norman MacCaig was there, and
someone I can't remember now, and Sylvia Plath, and Ted
Hughes. I'd bought it for myself, but this was school, and there
was nowhere private to play it. Never mind, the others who
weren't interested would soon give up nagging about it, or go

away. But the first time I played it no one left. Everyone sat still and listened.

'Full Moon and Little Frieda' was one of the poems, and thirty years later I can't see it on the page without feeling that first pleasure-shock all over again – hearing Hughes's voice with its electrifying delicate force, seeing the moon rise over the yard behind the house (at least I suppose it's a yard behind the house), and the child pointing and calling out, and everything moving and suspended at one and the same time.

Our favourite poems are not necessarily those we think biggest or best. This one is not in the least grand, and certainly has no palpable design on us – but while it's the intimacy of the thing I especially love, I also admire the big reach it manages so modestly. It's not just that everything is held almost-still; it's that everything is reciprocal – or soon will be. The dog-bark and bucket-clank have become the evening, swallowing its open vowels in the snapping jaws of their consonants. The spider's web is about to receive the dew's touch. The first star is about to rise in the pail. The cows are capturing the hedges with their breath-lassoes – their bodies are boulder-solid and yet milk-filled.

And then we get to the child, little Frieda, and the moon. This is the great, triumphant reciprocity, in which the child understands the identity of something in nature, and nature recognizes, astonished, something in humanity.

Recognizes, that is, by stepping back 'like an artist'. Suddenly the poem goes beyond its geography without betraying or undermining anything it has already given us. In a phrase, a glance, a rush, it makes us think about the relationship between art and artist, artist and audience – and about how mirrors are held up to nature. It's a 'Full' poem which knows the value of things that are 'Little'. It's a moment withdrawn from history – and unearthly – yet tremulous with the enormous pressure of history, and absolutely involved with the earth.

It's in *Wodwo*, which came out in 1967, and like everything else in that collection, it meets the charge and challenge of its time with a marvellously direct indirection.

MARTIN BOOTH

Journeying to 'Sunday'

21 August 1967. Monday. Severe tropical storm Kate was lashing Hong Kong. In readiness for a day of enforced domesticity, I had gone across to Swindon Bookshop in Lock Road in Kowloon on the Saturday evening before, specifically to purchase a book with which to kill the predicted storm hours.

The book I bought was *Wodwo*.

In those days, I was pretending to be a poet and had recently been voted in as secretary of the Poets' Workshop, formerly The Group, of which Ted Hughes had been a seminal member. Over that time, I'd met Ted twice but only in passing: once through the Workshop at a reading at the Poetry Society in Earl's Court Square and once in the company of my mentor, Edmund Blunden, at a reception in the British Museum. I already owned *Lupercal* and *The Hawk in the Rain* and had greatly anticipated the publication of this third full collection but hadn't been able to afford it when it was published in London in the late spring: I needed a stint of university holiday money-earning as a journalist before I could possess it.

It had been a temptation not to open the book on the night I bought it. I'd already had what I thought was a taster in the form of Alan Tarling's recent Poet & Printer booklet, *Scapegoats and Rabies*, and was ready for more: in the event, the poem was omitted from the collection. I sat at the bar in The Professional Club with the volume wrapped in a paper bag next to my glass of

[33]

San Mig lager. The place was not as salubrious as it sounds: it was in effect a dusk-'til-dawn drinking dive and knocking shop frequented almost exclusively by stringers, journalists and European police officers in Wanchai, the district being at the time at the height of its Suzie Wong bar era. Several times, the bar girls badgered me about it.

'Why you no opung?'

'You got dirty book?'

'Why you got dirty book? Plenty dirty girl here for you. You no want book.'

Wodwo had cost me, I recall, HK$25. A quick-time with one of the mini-skirted minions – cheongsams were out of fashion by then – was twenty bucks.

I resisted, as the saying went, both book and butt.

There was no temptation to read on the Sunday. The tropical storm might have been brewing in the South China Sea but the political typhoon of the Cultural Revolution was already blowing hard across China. Riots were the order of the day and home-made nail bombs were appearing on the streets, maiming children in tram queues and killing passers-by. I spent the day in the Foreign Correspondents' Club (watering hole but definitely *not* a knocking shop) waiting for action to cover and following it when it came. By nightfall, I had written my copy, dictated it to London or Washington, was exhausted and in no mood to read.

On Monday morning, the skies were gunboat grey and the rain rose vertically up the mountainside below my window. Every now and then, a tree branch went by in defiance of gravity. When the wind gusted, the window glass bowed inwards, distorting the reflection in it like a fun-fair mirror. The nail-bombers were off the streets. The Little Red Book mantra-chanters had temporarily abandoned their 24–hour demo-cum-vigil at the gates of Government House. I sat at my writing desk looking out over Deepwater Bay and opened the book at random.

Page 21: 'Ghost Crabs'. Instantly, I was back on the beach at Cheung Sha Wan, now being swamped by a heavy sea. It was night and the crabs almost glowed, their legs the radium hands of my battered red leather travelling clock, counting off crustacean half-lives in ticks of radioactive seconds.

This is the thing about Ted's work. No matter who you are or where you are or where you've been, the poems always mean something. Maybe subliminal, maybe immediate, maybe disguised, but always there. His writing has the ability not to suspend disbelief but extend belief. If ever there was a transport of (or to) delight, it is the poetry of Ted Hughes . . .

Shut the book and opened again around page 65. It was a shock. Truly. I remember the feeling now, opening the book again to write this little memoir. Apart from the kiddies' books, a mannerless monster and neatly crafted Kiplingesque creation tales, I'd no idea Ted wrote – could write – adult prose. Turned to the start of the story.

'Sunday'.

I'd never been to Yorkshire. It was a foreign landscape. And Michael's childhood was as alien to me as mine in China would have been to him tucked into the granite security of a valley in the Pennines. Yet the story took me by the balls and carried me from the tumult of a tropical storm to the white sun-warmed bench outside Top Wharf Pub. For twenty minutes, there was no howling wind, no rain bubbling through a crack in the Crittal iron window frame, no puddle spreading on the parquet floor. I was lost in the company of a small boy and a pretty girl, a game of bowls and a walk along the towpath where the banks of the canal had fallen in and surrendered to rank weeds.

And I was there when Billy Red appeared, downed his pint, took a leak and searched for rats in the pub's outhouses. I heard the rat in the cage scream like tearing tin and I listened as Billy Red flailed rat legs and tail against his cheeks.

Each paragraph held me spellbound. This was prose such as I'd never seen, a true – almost mystical – synthesis of all the command poetry demands of diction married to the rigid dictates of narrative. I'd stop and re-read a phrase: 'the smoke dragging off the chimneys like a tearing fleece' and the 'Aunt-infested

Sunday tea'. Billy Red's raw, 'flea-bitten look of a red hen' and his 'wrinkled, neglected fifty-year-old face shrunk on its small skull'. This was language working hard and winning. When Michael left his ginger beer untouched and ran off home, full tilt, I saw him go and followed breathless in his footsteps.

In those minutes of reading, I had come to realize just what language could do if you fired and forged and hit it hard enough. This was no mere story-telling. This was the craft of Beowulf and Piers the Plowman honed to the nth degree for a reader – or listener, for the language rang like the spoken word off the page – in the middle of the twentieth century.

The story done, I peered out into the grey, flat light of the storm but I was somewhere else, somewhere I'd never been before – but where I've been many times since in Ted's company.

In 1984, I was hired to do a writer-in-residence stint at the Arvon Foundation at Lumb Bank, below Heptonstall and the land of Elmet. This is Ted's home territory, where he grew up and where I knew I was near the genesis of the story. It was summer, the air warm on the harmless – yet no longer spotless – church-going slopes of the story, but edged with chill down in the valley shadows.

It was Sunday. I walked down the path beside Colden Water to Hebden Bridge. Small knots of elderly folk were clustered round the church. Along the streets, others walked slowly on in twos or threes to chapel. A train rattled by on its way from Manchester to Leeds.

For an hour I wandered up and down the valley, along the banks of the River Calder. I may have unknowingly seen Michael: in truth, I probably saw many of him in his dark Sunday suit with a sober tie and a white shirt and a starched collar and a Methodist stoop curved by labour, prayer and piety. I didn't find Top Wharf Pub or any hostelry that might conceivably have once been it.

And there was no Billy Red.

Or was there?

It matters not. I shall never need to shake his hand. Through Ted, I've seen him shake a rat to death in his teeth, as real as this page is printed, and that's enough.

W. S. MERWIN

'Pibroch'

_____

The sea cries with its meaningless voice
Treating alike its dead and its living,
Probably bored with the appearance of heaven
After so many millions of nights without sleep,
Without purpose, without self-deception.

Stone likewise. A pebble is imprisoned
Like nothing in the Universe.
Created for black sleep. Or growing
Conscious of the sun's red spot occasionally,
Then dreaming it is the foetus of God.

Over the stone rushes the wind
Able to mingle with nothing,
Like the hearing of the blind stone itself.
Or turns, as if the stone's mind came feeling
A fantasy of directions.

Drinking the sea and eating the rock
A tree struggles to make leaves –
An old woman fallen from space
Unprepared for these conditions.
She hangs on, because her mind's gone completely.

Minute after minute, aeon after aeon,
Nothing lets up or develops.

And this is neither a bad variant nor a tryout.
This is where the staring angels go through.
This is where all the stars bow down.

It is a startling poem to me still, after all the years since it first
rose from the page in front of me. In fact as startling as ever, in
spite of the number of times I have been through it, reading it,
then 'knowing' it in the way one thinks one knows a poem
because one remembers it word by word. What continues to be
startling after all that is perhaps poetry itself, what one hopes for
from poetry and occasionally finds in a poem, passage, line –
sometimes discovering it later after having missed it at other
turns of one's life.

Not the case for me with this one, and I remember clearly the
first time I read it, standing in the morning sunlight in an
apartment in New York, and going on standing to read it again,
ringing from the first time, and then sitting down to keep reading
it, hovering over line after line, listening to how it happened.

Why this poem in particular? I had loved Ted's poetry since I
read *The Hawk in the Rain*, five or six years earlier. Poems of his
from that collection and later had opened up in front of me with
that chthonian skirl, those blunt rhythms and mallet phrases in
their rushing current of sombre feeling. The title had nothing to
do with it, to begin with. At that first reading I was not aware of
what Pibroch, or pibroch, meant. I imagined it must be a place,
somewhere on the coast of Britain. I had grown familiar with the
poem before I looked up the title and discovered, along with the
ironies of my own ignorance, some of the ironies of the word's
ancestry, which was not – as the sound of it and something in the
sound of the poem had led me to imagine – Celtic but English,
from 'pipe', and before that from Latin *pipare*. A 'chirp', that
long ago. A brief little thing. Making its way across Europe,
becoming caught in the circling movements of flocks, the
measures of Pan and his progeny, arriving among Celtic tongues
to be used to name a sound of instruments that may have been
there for a long time already with their shapes and their sound

described by earlier words, now lost to us. Pibroch: 'a kind of traditional bagpipe music', the current definitions agree, in the form of 'variations on a dirge or martial theme'.

But I expect it was no published definition but a familiar acquaintance with the present charge of the word which provided the sense and resonance that would claim this poem. If I understand how the word works here, one of the things it speaks for is the single continuing note, audible or not, running through all the dimensions of the phenomenal world, through time, space, existence, never broken, varying endlessly, never repeating, turning, renewing, accompanying, unravelling, at once quickening and terrifying. Understood in this way, it represents the core strand of the great theme, however that may be conceived of or designated, respected or avoided.

And the tone, the diction, the rush of the poem become a kind of articulation and manifestation of this pervasive continuo. I had read it a number of times before its perfectly evident division into successive parts emerged for me from what had seemed at first to be a single unbroken cadenza. The changes are there, the variations on the dirge, the meaningless cry of the sea, the stone's black dreaming sleep, the wind's fantasy, the old woman tree hanging on. What they come to is what they have been all along: aspects of the theme of immediate encounter, unique and without appeal, not only beyond but underneath reason, recognized intuitively and unquestionably as the eternal present. It is the encounter, the instantaneous recognition that we describe elsewhere with such words as 'divine' and 'mysterium'. It is the uninterrupted, ungraspable source without which there would be no meaning and no life. It is also, of course, the well-spring of music, of the Muses, of poetry, the origin and current of language, and of the recognition that sustains it. That, I think, is what the title has to do with the content of this singular poem, which in turn seems to me to be an archetype or hologram for Hughes's poetry as a whole, for the cast of his sensibility and imagination.

And the voice in this poem is up to the theme and its awesome grandeur. Again and again in these twenty-five lines the images turn and emerge out of themselves, maintaining the starting presence of the whole poem. It seems to by-pass modern critical concerns about what may be called concrete and what is abstract and to engage, in metaphor after metaphor, in identification of human experience with the phenomenal world, something which the theme itself tends to suggest and perhaps demand. The sea 'cries with its meaningless voice' – every word in the image assumes that metaphoric identification, without which the sea has no voice and cannot cry, and the notion of meaning is meaningless. The pebble is 'imprisoned / Like nothing in the Universe', and the words 'like nothing' make the metaphor and the simile inside it ricochet and echo, for only an articulate something can conceive of a something like nothing. The manifestations of the phenomenal world appear as recurrent forms of human consciousness, of the continuing imagination.

After the rising current of variations the last lines gather the turns and run of the whole poem into a high finality that leaves everything wide open, which is also what it is about, saying 'this, all this, is unique; this is the only time; and there *can* be no other.' This is not

> . . . a tryout.
> This is where the staring angels go through.
> This is where all the stars bow down.

It is a daring statement, a wording that seems to articulate the impossible (which again may be what we hope for from poetry), a recognition that is chilling and exhilarating, dangerous and transparent. It projects a harsh view of existence, reminiscent of Schopenhauer's worst of all possible worlds. It would be simply bleak if the power of the language itself, of the poetry, did not present it in a current of dark joy.

I have been grateful for this poem since that first reading.

JAMIE MCKENDRICK

Hurrying through the Underworld: 'Second Glance at a Jaguar'

Skinful of bowls he bowls them,
The hip going in and out of joint, dropping the spine
With the urgency of his hurry
Like a cat going along under thrown stones, under cover,
Glancing sideways, running
Under his spine. A terrible, stump-legged waddle
Like a thick Aztec disemboweller,
Club-swinging, trying to grind some square
Socket between his hind legs round,
Carrying his head like a brazier of spilling embers,
And the black bit of his mouth, he takes it
Between his back teeth, he has to wear his skin out,
He swipes a lap at the water-trough as he turns,
Swivelling the ball of his heel on the polished spot,
Showing his belly like a butterfly.
At every stride he has to turn a corner
In himself and correct it. His head
Is like the worn down stump of another whole jaguar,
His body is just the engine shoving it forward,
Lifting the air up and shoving on under,
The weight of his fangs hanging the mouth open,
Bottom jaw combing the ground. A gorged look,
Gangster, club-tail lumped along behind gracelessly,
He's wearing himself to heavy ovals,

Muttering some mantra, some drum-song of murder
To keep his rage brightening, making his skin
Intolerable, spurred by the rosettes, the Cain-brands,
Wearing the spots off from the inside,
Rounding some revenge. Going like a prayer-wheel,
The head dragging forward, the body keeping up,
The hind legs lagging. He coils, he flourishes
The blackjack tail as if looking for a target,
Hurrying through the underworld, soundless.

As far back as we care to go, in poems, in dreams and in life, big cats mean business and threaten our safety. Jeremiah's prophesy plays on that dread: 'Wherefore a lion out of the forest shall slay them, and a wolf of the evenings shall spoil them, a leopard shall watch over their cities.' And Dante employs these same three animals to impede his pilgrim's progress, allowing for the small change of leopard to *lonza,* a creature wearing a 'gay pelt' and known only to medieval bestiaries. In 'Poetry and Violence', his eloquent essay-reply to questions by Ekbert Faas, Ted Hughes refers to Blake's 'Tyger' and Yeats's 'Second Coming' in connection with his own two jaguar poems. Both Blake's and Yeats's creations are instinct with a physical, psychic and, as Hughes makes clear, political violence.

Hughes's poem 'Second Glance at a Jaguar' revisits the subject of his own poem 'The Jaguar' in a darker and more urgent spirit, and is an heir to all these. It breathes the same kind of menace as Jeremiah. Where his earlier poem had annulled the cage – 'Over the cage floor the horizons come', implying the rondure of the whole earth – the later 'glance' reveals a kind of obsessive, fateful, almost thuggish fury. This poem seems to enter still deeper into, to get further under the skin of the animal as it tries 'to grind some square / Socket between his hind legs round.' The cumulative effect of all those verbs of grinding and wearing out ('he has to wear his skin out') and wearing down and swivelling and rounding is like a ghost-dance performed in a primitive stone-tumbling drum. If we compare it to Rilke's 'The Panther', another poem with which it has some kinship, we see that it offers an altogether more disturbing, less aestheticized experience. One aspect of the disturbance is the way that the animal is made to mirror back to us various vicious forms of human behaviour – 'gangster', 'dream of murder', 'Rounding some revenge' all are anthropomorphically insistent, as is the more culturally specific reference to Aztec ritual sacrifice. It's this capacity to disturb that brings the poem far closer to the heat of Blake's 'Tyger'.

Hughes's jaguar is much more closely, naturalistically, and, if the word doesn't sound too cosy, empathetically observed than Blake's 'fearful' emblem that leaps at us with its incantatory rhythms and repetitions. Of Blake's poem, Hughes writes: 'Blake saw his Tyger in a "vision" and tried to make sense of it by controlling it, yoking it with the Lamb (Christ, its apparent antithesis) and the God of Job'. This idea of control, the taming of the tiger, seems to me to overlook the cruel-cunning intent behind Blake's poem, its polemical depth-charge that occurs in the line 'Did He who made the Lamb make Thee?' Blake is questioning the kind of Christian cosmology that excludes the terrifying evidence of the creation by lifting up the image of the lamb. But Hughes's poem shows how well he understands that intent as, incidentally, does his account of his own poem 'Thrushes' in the same essay. The caged animal, although subtracted from the natural order, still belongs to it, in a way that its captors, to their cost, do not.

'Second Glance at a Jaguar' can be seen as Hughes's 'The Second Coming', his own 'vast image out of *Spiritus Mundi*'. As Yeats's poem begins with the falcon 'Turning and turning in the widening gyre', Hughes begins with a perception of roundness and velocity: 'Skinful of bowls he bowls them', and follows the earlier poem's taste for present participles. The whole poem worries at the jaguar's internal anatomical geometry; it assumes something of the same 'urgency of his hurry', discarding in the process one shape after another just as the jaguar itself seems to be refining its movements towards a perfect (imaginary) kill. The spherical and circular images give way finally to 'heavy ovals'. These egg-shaped birth- and death-bearing bones, which the jaguar has worn himself down to, subliminally evoke Yeats's sphinx-like beast which 'Slouches towards Bethlehem to be born'. But what does the jaguar give birth to? Itself – its head is a whole other reproduction of itself, a smaller, carved, or rather honed down version:

> His head
> Is like the worn down stump of another whole jaguar,
> His body is just the engine shoving it forward,
> Lifting the air up and shoving it under.

It has duplicated its overworld self in the underworld. This isn't so much the human, criminal underworld that the poem has also evoked, but a mythical underworld which is no other than the human psyche.

Hughes's tautological and hyperbolic imagination is at its most triumphant when dealing with this moment of definition in which, as Hopkins puts it, 'each mortal thing . . . Deals out that being indoors each one dwells; / Selves – goes itself; *myself* it speaks and spells, / Crying *What I do is me: for that I came*'. It is one of Hughes's most characteristic tropes – the point at which a mortal thing 'Selves – goes itself', where it sheds all the approximations that the poem has used to approach or stalk it, the point at which Hughes can declare, as he does in 'Pibroch',

> And this is neither a bad variant nor a tryout.
> This is where the staring angels go through.
> This is where all the stars bow down.

At one level the naturalistic observation in Hughes's animal poems may camouflage the supernatural drive behind the writing. The poem demands that we read it both as perceived reality and as cosmology. 'He coils, he flourishes / The blackjack tail as if looking for a target' and that target is the human psyche which would prefer to shut out this image of power. The threat which the jaguar poses 'Hurrying through the underworld, soundless' is one which the reader has to answer, just as he must in reading 'Tyger' or 'The Second Coming'. With Jeremiah it says 'a leopard shall watch over your cities'.

Many have noticed that Hughes's natural world is over-red, his seas incarnadined:

> The deeps are cold:
> In that darkness camaraderie does not hold:
> Nothing touches but, clutching, devours.

> ('Relic')

Kropotkin might point out a few examples of mutual aid among the species. Even moray eels can be stroked, as divers have discovered, without biting off the hand that does so. But if Hughes doesn't inhabit a Peaceable Kingdom, his poems insist on the need not to settle for a falsifying world view which gives us teddy bears whilst it devastates the habitat both of the actual jaguar and the mythical *lonza*.

PETER REDGROVE

'Gnat-Psalm'

When the gnats dance at evening
Scribbling on the air, sparring sparely,
Scrambling their crazy lexicon,
Shuffling their dumb Cabala,
Under leaf shadow

Leaves only leaves
Between them and the broad swipes of the sun
Leaves muffling the dusty stabs of the late sun
From their frail eyes and crepuscular temperaments

Dancing
Dancing
Writing on the air, rubbing out everything they write
Jerking their letters into knots, into tangles
Everybody everybody else's yoyo

Immense magnets fighting around a centre

Not writing and not fighting but singing
That the cycles of this Universe are no matter
That they are not afraid of the sun
That the one sun is too near
It blasts their song, which is of all the suns
That they are their own sun
Their own brimming over

At large in the nothing
Their wings blurring the blaze
Singing

That they are the nails
In the dancing hands and feet of the gnat-god
That they hear the wind suffering
Through the grass
And the evening tree suffering

The wind blowing with long cat-gut cries
And the long roads of dust
Dancing in the wind
The wind's dance, the death-dance, entering the mountain
And the cow dung villages huddling to dust

But not the gnats, their agility
Has outleaped that threshold
And hangs them a little above the claws of the grass
Dancing
Dancing
In the glove shadows of the sycamore

A dance never to be altered
A dance giving their bodies to be burned

And their mummy faces will never be used

Their little bearded faces
Weaving and bobbing on the nothing
Shaken in the air, shaken, shaken
And their feet dangling like the feet of victims

O little Hasids
Ridden to death by your own bodies
Riding your bodies to death
You are the angels of the only heaven!

And God is an almighty Gnat!
You are the greatest of all the galaxies!

My hands fly in the air, they are follies
My tongue hangs up in the leaves
My thoughts have crept into crannies

Your dancing

Your dancing

Rolls my staring skull slowly away into outer space.

I think of 'Gnat-Psalm' as the flip side of 'The Thought-Fox'. The fox is bone and flesh before it is a printed page, it is concentrated, intense, egoistic; the gnats are horny ampoules, brimming with elixir; self-forgetful, they have the sun running in their veins and by kinship with the sun are a portion of deity. They, like the thought-fox, are writing, but writing as a cabala of improvisation in their dance. The fox is a stealthy phallus; the gnats are stating a continual orgasm of life. As an animal, the fox can live and die, insects however metamorphose continually and these are rapidly becoming the sun itself.

Cabala is what you might call Solid God or Physiological Theology. It is linguistic yoga and improvisation by rules. You juggle with the letters and the letters become God and answer you with creative intelligence instead of the randomness you might expect. We come across the gnat chorus in its state as a place where something is always being made. It is spiritual brownian movement – the particles move of themselves and reveal invisible forces. The lexicon answers back.

I first met Ted Hughes in his last year at Cambridge. There was a tall wooden staircase to his rooms. A strange yowling was coming out of this doorway of a kind that I had never known before – I was not at that time musical. I knocked and entered. In the brightly lit room a hand-wound gramophone was playing a black disc – this was the yowling. My puzzlement was complete. Hughes's own physical presence was also of a kind I had never encountered before. It was decisive – very few people in my experience had the ability of showing by their physique a kind of knowledge. This was cabalistic. 'This is Beethoven's last quartet,' he said, understanding that I had never before heard it: 'It is as if the whole of the music is crushed into the first few bars, which are then unravelled.' I think this was how he explained that yowling, which indeed had now turned into an angelic singing. 'Look! This is the author' – and he hooked a frowning kindly plaster mask off the wall. 'This is how he walked' – and he waddled this face towards me at chest-level. 'This was his height and how he walked.'

This meeting was for me in continuum with his poems. In contrast to the Cambridge atmosphere which was ironic and provisional, his poems had knowledge or arrived at knowledge. He was one of the few people who knew or sensed how much had to go into a poem before the words transformed into another mode of being that was poetry, though like the gnats they were dancing and singing in the course of the poem and casting a light that was both individual and universal. There was a 'crossing' in which the mode of understanding changed, as described by the American critic Harold Bloom in writing about Wallace Stevens (in *The Poems of Our Climate*). You arrive at an understanding while at the same time being companioned by that understanding. Something real has arrived. There is real presence. The gnats are transforming, their song is altering their body which is a god-cloud of minute particulars, a hypnotic cloud which is a poem capable of generating poetry.

I choose this poem, therefore, among this towering oeuvre for its prophetic quality – that this is the creative mode of thinking that may be the way poetry stripped of its ironic inheritance, gentility, all unnecessary defences, may now be going. There is more than an acknowledgement of this from other quarters. Sadie Plant's 1997 book *zeros + ones* is one. She writes of the beginning of a process which abandons the model of 'the organic body, organized with survival as its goal' – as it might be the Thought-Fox – in favour of a diagram of fluid sex – she is also quoting Baudrillard – 'Flows of intensity, their fluids, their fibres, their continuums and conjunctions of affects, the wind, fine segmentation, microperceptions have replaced the world of the subject' – as it might be the Thought-Fox – now there are 'acentred systems . . . in which communication runs from any neighbour to any other. . . we too are flows of matter and energy (sunlight, oxygen, water, protein . . .).' Human bodies also 'imply a multiplicity of molecular combinations bringing into play not only the man in the woman and the woman in the man, but the relation of each to the animal, the plant, etc'; 'Every unified body conceals a crowd . . .'

Plant's subject is the weblike, loomlike interweaving of human with non-human, the texture of mind in the machinery of the world. People are asking still 'what is the use of poetry?' not seeing that the poetic process is the basic process of implicated mind and body – the immune system turns out to be the dream system as well, according to recent science, and there are two basic operations in the physiology of the brain in which are constellated two varieties of personality – the slow waking ego, hunting its purposes – again as it might be the Thought-Fox – and the glittering archives of a being very like a guardian angel that acts with supernatural speed and forgets nothing, as the gnats preserve knowledge with their cabala. Hughes was one of the poets who knew this and from his struggles made such affirmations which are now beginning to be ratified by foxy science.

Now the man has gone, but his discoveries remain, generating life which is poetry.

WENDY COPE

The Iron Man and the 'Moon-Hops'

────────

Very early on in my career as a primary school teacher, I read Ted
Hughes's poem 'View of a Pig' to a class of eight and nine-year-
olds. Some of them may have enjoyed it but what I remember is
that one little girl had to leave the room and lie down because the
poem had made her feel sick.

That was the only bad experience that came of using Hughes's
work in the classroom. The good experiences, over a period of
fifteen years, were many and various. Hughes's importance and
distinction as a children's author are overshadowed by his other
achievements – the more so because many literary people have a
dismissive attitude to children's books. In primary schools –
where I sometimes had colleagues who hadn't heard of Larkin or
Heaney – Ted Hughes has been a big name for the last thirty
years, for reasons that have nothing to do with his books for
grown ups.

The Iron Man was first published in 1968, not long after I
began teaching. As I read the opening pages, I recognized that
this was going to be a hit with my class. On the first page there is
a compelling description of the Iron Man, employing similes that
relate the giant to a child's world – his head is 'shaped like a
dustbin but as big as a bedroom', his eyes are 'like headlamps'.
The reader doesn't have to wait for the action to begin. On the
second page the protagonist topples over a cliff and falls to bits.
In a marvellous passage on the fourth page the bits start putting

themselves together again, 'But as soon as the eye and the hand got together the eye looked at the hand. The hand stood up on three fingers and its thumb, and craned its forefinger like a long nose. It felt around. It touched the eye. Gleefully it picked up the eye, and tucked it under its middle finger.' I read *The Iron Man*, a chapter a day, to several classes, always in tough inner-city schools, and they always loved it. As the book's popularity grew I read it less often, because last year's teacher had usually got in first.

Of Hughes's poems for children, the one I used most often was the quatrain called 'Moon-Hops'. It begins, 'Hops are a menace on the moon, a nuisance crop.' And ends, wonderfully, with this long line: 'Clip-clop at first, then flip-flop, then slip-slop, till finally they droopily drop and all their pods pop.' I don't know what becomes of moon-hops in today's primary schools but back in the era when creativity was a buzzword they were a stimulus for work in art, dance, drama, and music. I have still got, somewhere, a tape of a child reading the poem, while the rest of the group do interesting things with xylophones, cymbals and woodblocks.

Doing this kind of work with children helped me discover a creative side of myself. I began writing poems, and aspired to write better ones. As I worked at it in my spare time, I often thought about my favourite Ted Hughes children's book, the collection of stories called *How The Whale Became*. The creatures in these stories practise becoming what they want to be. 'The ones that wanted to become lions practised at being lions – and by and by, sure enough, they began to turn into lions.' Some creatures, such as Donkey and Hyena, don't practise being what they want to be. They merely dream about it, and have to settle for less. When I caught myself practising to become a couch-potato or a workaholic teacher, it was salutary to remember them.

I re-read the book recently, while editing an anthology of bedtime stories. The one I chose to include is 'How The Elephant Became', the story of a clumsy, unhappy creature who becomes a hero, and then disappears into the forest. 'Ask any of the animals and they will tell you: Though he is shy, he is the strongest, the cleverest and the kindest of all the animals . . . We would make him our king if we could get him to wear a crown.' It was never easy to read that paragraph aloud. But it probably doesn't do any harm for children to see their teacher getting out her handkerchief at the end of an especially moving story.

SUSAN HILL

Moon-Bells

━━━━━━

Ted Hughes is a fathoms-deep poet. Some would say unfathomable. His imagery and the myths in which his work is steeped, the work's frame of reference, all of these are fathoms deep. Every poem, every stanza, every line, almost every word, and another new meaning. His surface may sometimes seem knowable but what lies beneath can scarcely be trawled.

As a result, he has brought out the very worst in some of his critics, exegesists and commentators. Probably unable to fathom it all themselves – and how would they? – they become desperate and add their own two-penn'orth of dark unfathomability, grow images on his images, myths on his myths and explanations on his absence of them. So – we believe that Ted Hughes is a 'difficult poet'. In the sense of being unfathomable, so he is – so is Donne, and so is W. H. Auden. Only bad poets are easy, the 'what-you-see-is-what-you-get' sort of writers.

Yet the greatest poets, though ultimately unfathomable, are accessible too; that is, there is a door by which we can enter their work. We can read, mark and inwardly digest their poems, if only in part. Their language and their rhythms sing to us, their images and metaphors illuminate the dark corners of our lives. If it were not so, what would be the point of them? (Always supposing they do not merely to sing to themselves like little children and lunatics, which would be perfectly in order.)

So, the poetry may be difficult but never impossible.

That is certainly as true of Ted Hughes as of any. He is a poet to chew on: sinewy, dense, crammed with reference and cross reference which taxes our thinking, makes us dig not only into the poems themselves but into the recesses of our own memories, reading and imaginations.

Yet there is also a clear, plain, strong, essential simplicity about his work. It is to do with his being a countryman, I think, and a North countryman at that, even though he lived for years in Devon.

His critics, and especially the more convoluted, arcane and abstruse among them, have not always seen the wood for the trees. They have not really understood the complex simplicity, and one of the reasons is that they have not considered his poetry for children – indeed, it is rarely so much as mentioned save in passing, and never taken seriously. Well, that it is par for the course. The children's poetry written by that other great contemporary poet, Charles Causley, has not been taken seriously either (except by the children themselves).

Both Causley and Ted Hughes have written some of their best poetry for the young. They do take the job seriously.

If you want to find a way into Hughes's work and begin to understand it well, begin with his poetry for children, and begin with the best, the slim collection *Moon-Bells*. In those pages are all his strengths, almost all the themes that run through the whole body of his work, all his recurrent mighty images; they share his moral stance and are permeated by his philosophy, and above all they reveal his genius with words and the rhythms of words. There is a wonderful poetic playfulness that is also deadly serious, but it is somehow all simplified, crystallized, transparent, though the depths that lie behind these magical, haunting poems are still – well, unfathomable.

Too often poetry for children is not poetry at all, it is doggerel, and much contemporary verse-writing for the young is not merely bad beyond belief, it is patronizing, packed with ingratiating references to what the writers think the young say, feel, and are interested in. It makes an embarrassing show of being streetwise, endeavours desperately to share in the world picture of the young. It is a doomed enterprise, of course. Children see through all this perfectly well. Once you are old you can never go back, nor should you try. They have changed all the signs round. You can no more share in their world or see ours through their eyes than you can keep up with the rapid changes in their patois.

One thing is certain. The young, even the young unread, respond to poetry.

Poetry, not the garbage that is so often foisted on them. They respond nakedly to the best. To Ted Hughes. He knew that it is unnecessary, as it is undesirable, to talk down or water down because the mighty themes and images which are his everyday coin are those to which the young respond; the things that matter to him matter to them: death, war, violence, victims, the desecration of the natural world, cruelty in the animal kingdom and cruelty to it. The darkness at the heart of things, the mysterious, the alien, the bizarre. The casual, surreal juxtapositions of life.

It is all there in *Moon-Bells* and one of the most exciting things about it is the language and the way that these great themes and these minute, deadly bullets of accurate observation and comment are so ringingly caught and held by nothing more violent than words.

Children like their poetry to be confrontational, to meet big themes, big notions, big ideas, head on. Lyricism and subtlety make little appeal. Hughes knows this. Some of the poems in *Moon-Bells* are about death, blood and predators and there are no holds barred; they are direct poems though rarely simple and certainly never simplistic.

There are also wonderful half-surreal, half-magical poems, the safe stuff of fancy and fantasy out of which Edward Lear formed his best verses, yet with a darker meaning than 'The Jumblies' or 'The Dong with the Luminous Nose'. Delve into the best of these and you delve into layers of mist and smoke and mirrors shimmering with meaning upon concealed meaning which changes even as you look at it. A poem like 'Earth Moon' is serious, frightening, a warning of a poem, ominous and eerie – disturbing as moonlight and as beautiful.

An understanding of poetry can be taught. The young (and the old too, for that matter) can be helped to a greater understanding of a poem's meaning and things that conspire to express – and sometimes also to conceal – that meaning. There is so much potential for fruitful discussion, for delving about in *Moon-Bells*, so much to get one's teeth into. But the surface is seductive, too, glittering with intelligence, vivid with lightening flashes of imagery, fraught with possibilities, beckoning you in. And then there are the perfect little phrases, apparently so nonchalantly placed, that take the breath away.

If I were capable of being a teacher these are the poems I would bring into the classroom with me. And although lyricism – the soppy, girlish face of poetry – might be scorned, in practice, the beauty of the language would steal up and overcome the young ones like a spell, for indeed they are spellbinding, these *Moon-Bells* poems. They are also strange, odd, bizarre, and those things are very readily taken on board by children. Read *Moon-Bells* as an adult and you find that being spellbound still comes naturally.

SEAMUS HEANEY

Omen and Amen: On 'Littleblood'

———

After Ted's death there was a temptation to change what follows,
perhaps even to change the choice of poem to 'The Day He
Died', which now seems such a true self-elegy. But then I
thought, so be it. Amen. Let what was written stand.

> O littleblood, hiding from the mountains in the mountains
> Wounded by stars and leaking shadow
> Eating the medical earth.
>
> O littleblood, little boneless, little skinless
> Ploughing with a linnet's carcase
> Reaping the wind and threshing the stones.
>
> O littleblood, drumming in a cow's skull
> Dancing with a gnat's feet
> With an elephant's nose with a crocodile's tail.
>
> Grown so wise grown so terrible
> Sucking death's mouldy tits.
>
> Sit on my finger, sing in my ear, O littleblood.

Littleblood. The name could belong to oral tradition, to fairytale,
to the world of *A Midsummer Night's Dream*. It could be a
cognate of Peaseblossom and Mustardseed, an escapee from the
conversation of Peter Quince or Robin Starveling. Like the
names of Shakespeare's fairies (and the fact that Littleblood eats

'the medical earth' confirms this impression) it could be the name of an ingredient in folk medicine, the requisite gout or smear from the cut neck of a bird or the pricked thumb of a spinster. It feels as if it might belong to a whole system of story or lore, and it would be easy enough to mistake the poem where it appears for one translated from some collection of material preserved more for its anthropological than its literary interest.

And of course the poem does belong in just such a collection. In the volume named for him, it is the last of the songs Crow sings, and the tenderest, and follows immediately upon the tundra cheeps of 'Two Eskimo Songs'. Reading it after the 'Bessemer glare' of all the other poems in *Crow* is like being exposed to some kind of healing ray. Like 'eating the medical earth' and finding in it at least a memory of its pre-atomic-age goodness. And this tenderness is probably why Ted always read it with particular delicacy and intensity, articulating the *t* of 'eating' and the *d* and hard *c* of 'medical' so finely and distinctly they were like the small twig-bones of a bird's skeleton, a robin's, say, since it was a robin's breast I glimpsed – and the poem's mention of a linnet has not dislodged the image – when my mind's eye first blinked at the sight and sound of Littleblood, the name.

Littleblood, the name, only the name . . . To echo Edward Thomas is pertinent because this is to some extent a poem like 'Adlestrop', a poem where the lyric tremor of the word releases forces well below the surface. And there is another link between the two poets insofar as both are haunted by the shadow of the war in Flanders, and through that preoccupation with the British Expeditionary Force, they are shadowed too by earlier expeditions such as the one that culminated at Agincourt. In fact, Littleblood could just as well be found among the 'dramatis personae' of one of Shakespeare's history plays, although he would probably fit in better with the pathetic flibbertigibbets of Falstaff's 'mortal men, mortal men' in *Henry IV, Part II* than with the blooded soldiers of *Henry V*: he belongs more in the company of Mouldy and Shadow and Wart and Feeble and Bullcalf than of Gower and Fluellen and Macmorris.

But then, how can we be sure that Littleblood is a 'he'? There is an element of androgyny about this 'little boneless, little skinless', something pre-pubertal and Ariel-like. Coming at the end of a book dedicated 'In memory of Assia and Shura', this wisp of a ghost dancer could easily be conflated with the shade of the girl-child who in the meantime has 'Grown so wise grown so terrible / Sucking death's mouldy tits.' Certainly the poem is set in the aftermath of traumatic, even cataclysmic events: the reapers of the whirlwind have prayed for the mountains to fall upon them, and now, 'hiding from the mountains in the mountains' something stirs in the eyehole of a cow's skull, a kind of post-nuclear fledgeling, something as frail as the second coming of pity, that 'naked, new-born babe / Striding the blast', an image which Ted reads (in *Shakespeare and the Goddess of Complete Being*) as proleptic of 'a new kind of agonizing transformation'.

This transformation he characterizes as a shift in the plane of understanding from the tragic to the transcendental, and I have always tended to read 'Littleblood' as an instance of just that kind of transition. It is as if, at the last moment, grace has entered into the Crow-cursed universe and a voice that had hitherto been as obsessive and self-flagellating as the Ancient Mariner's suddenly finds that it can pray. More than a quarter of a century before the publication of *Birthday Letters*, before the appearance of the poem 'Freedom of Speech', Littleblood is granted this little moment of epiphany, sitting on the poet's finger, singing in his ear, singing the song of both omen and amen.

The note of amen is proleptic: 'Littleblood' looks forward to 'Freedom of Speech', and says 'so be it', let Ariel perch on a knuckle and let the stars not wound but 'shake with laughter'. The note of omen, however, acknowledges that the under-standing behind all future poems is going to be darkened, and what gives 'Littleblood' its mysterious, votive power is the coexistence of this tragic understanding (which the last line of 'Freedom of Speech' cannot and will not repress) with other, more transcendent desires and realizations.

D. J. ENRIGHT

Crow: A Reading

———

Crow is the quintessence of Ted Hughes's writing; or, one might venture, a rumbustious caricature of it.

Death owns everything, 'Examination at the Womb-Door' tells us, the whole of earth, the whole of space; death is stronger than love and life. Is anything stronger than death? 'Me, evidently.' Evidently, in that Crow appears to get killed on occasion, even 'blasted to nothing', but always pops up again, full of disastrous vim. It's Crow who gives the human creation, or rather procreation, a kick-start when God falls asleep, exhausted by the problem of what to do with two bodies, one male, the other female. In another poem this uncouth Siva re-creates creation – with horrid consequences – by nailing heaven and earth together. (That no indication is given of how this is achieved is a mark of the most primitive form of creation myth.) The word 'Love' sticks in Crow's gullet. He isn't always *au fait* with what is going on; like some legendary figures, lords of misrule, he can fall victim to his own black jokes. In this, unlike the later vulture, whom Prometheus himself had to admire: 'It knew what it was doing' and 'It went on doing it' ('Prometheus on his Crag'). True, though, Crow goes on doing it, whatever it is; often, as with the vulture, it consists in tearing and devouring.

Humour or simple comedy helps to alleviate the mayhem; as in 'Apple Tragedy', which signals the invention of strong liquor, the beginnings of drunkenness, domestic disorder, and the eternal triangle. The pervasive violence erupts in 'Crow's Account of St George', more an account of Crow at play, one would say, than of the saint, unless the latter is on a very bad trip. And when man and woman fell on their knees before the serpent, Crow contemptuously grabbed it by the nape, 'beat the hell out of it, and ate it'. So 'A Horrible Religious Error' reports. But who was in what error? Perhaps we shouldn't question or strive to make sense of what is happening, much as we might like to. After all, Crow 'was what his brain could make nothing of' ('Crow's Playmates'). On the other hand, when 'Crow Goes Hunting' with his 'lovely pack' of words – plainly not those picturesque words in another poem, 'Waving their long tails in public / With their prostitute's exclamations' – there's no call for exegesis; the poem means what it says, says what it means, in the mode of the best nursery rhymes. And likewise, though decidedly not a story for the nursery, 'A Bedtime Story'.

As if Crow, his life and songs, weren't enough, its hero/villain crops up in various guises elsewhere in Hughes's work, earlier and later. The 'Hawk Roosting' observes, 'There is no sophistry in my body: / My manners are tearing off heads.' 'Esther's Tom-cat' takes the head clean off pullets, and is 'unkillable'. The 'Eagle' 'stamps his shaggy-trousered dance / On an altar of blood'. Even the thrushes are 'terrifying' (if only to the worms), while in a gentle or genial, amusing touch swifts are 'international mobsters'. A precursor is 'Theology', a calm, 'factual' rectification of events in Eden: Adam ate the apple, Eve ate Adam, the serpent ate Eve. We know what Crow is to do with the serpent. And 'Do Not Pick Up The Telephone' (in *Selected Poems 1957–81*) contends that death invented the telephone: 'O phone get out of my house / You are a bad god / . . . Do not lift your snake head in my house.' The poem is both violent and funny, as if a parody of *Crow*, the mythic manner applied to what is commonly reckoned a harmless necessary adjunct to everyday life.

'Crow realized there were two Gods – / One of them much bigger than the other' ('Crow's Theology'). An approximation, it

[63]

may seem, to the Manichaean picture of primeval and everlasting conflict between light and darkness, in which, here, Good or God comes off a bad second, there being so few signs of light. Crow has nothing of the desolate pride of Milton's Satan, or of the finesse and sophistication of Mephistopheles, that great literary seducer. (Hughes's serpent comes a little closer, but is still remote.) No matter how we conceive of the devil otherwise, we rather want him to be witty, ingenious, even (as in Goethe's view) a creative stimulus; at the very least someone who takes us humans seriously. Crow is elemental and inchoate, a warlord with a heavy-handed sense of humour, the bare bones of a largely unmediated myth; raw, not cooked. Though the hyenas in 'Crow's Elephant Totem Song' have 'their shame-flags tucked hard down / Over the gutsacks', and the tipsy serpent in 'Apple Tragedy' is 'curled up into a questionmark', the sequence is short on the intimate, telling detail, present in, say, 'A Haunting' and the Jaguar poems: 'The hip going in and out of joint, dropping the spine / With the urgency of his hurry.' Crow is a force, an act or accident of God, not an individual; and, in the terms in which Dr Johnson described the business of a poet, Hughes is not concerned to number the streaks of the tulip. And certainly not to humanize Crow.

Even though Crow has been put in a book, 'His wings are the stiff back of his only book, / Himself the only page – of solid ink.' Like Parolles, but with no hint of repentance, he could say, Simply the thing I am shall make me live.

LEONARD BASKIN
Six Crows

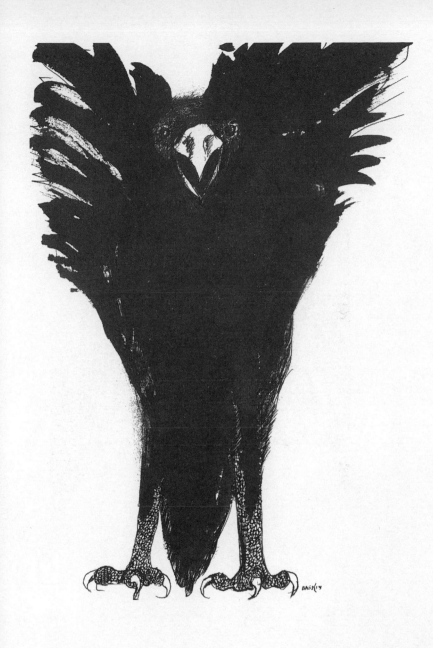

1978   Baskin

'A Cranefly in September'

She is struggling through grass-mesh – not flying,
her wide-winged, stiff, weightless basket-work of limbs
Rocking, like an antique wain, a top-heavy ceremonial cart
Across mountain summits
(Not planing over water, dipping her tail)
But blundering with long strides, long reachings, reelings
And ginger-glistening wings
From collision to collision.
Aimless in no particular direction,
Just exerting her last to escape out of the overwhelming
Of whatever it is, legs, grass,
The garden, the county, the country, the world –

Sometimes she rests long minutes in the grass forest
Like a fairytale hero, only a marvel can help her.
She cannot fathom the mystery of this forest
In which, for instance, this giant watches –
The giant who knows she cannot be helped in any way.

Her jointed bamboo fuselage,
Her lobster shoulders, and her face
Like a pinhead dragon, with its tender moustache,
And the simple colourless church windows of her wings
Will come to an end, in mid-search, quite soon.
Everything about her, every perfected vestment

Is already superfluous.
The monstrous excess of her legs and curly feet
Are a problem beyond her.
The calculus of glucose and chitin inadequate
To plot her through the infinities of the stems.

The frayed apple leaves, the grunting raven, the defunct
    tractor
Sunk in nettles, wait with their multiplications
Like other galaxies.
The sky's Northward September progression, the vast soft
    armistice,
Like an Empire on the move,
Abandons her, tinily embattled
With her cumbering limbs and cumbered brain.

In Hughes's nature poems – specially those in *Season Songs* – there is an intensity of seeing akin to the best work of John Clare. To see the natural world so closely and to be able to pass this information on to the less observant in a way that is memorable is one of his major gifts, and one that those of us whose vision is blunted by hurry or enclosed in an urban environment ought to be grateful for. In 'A Cranefly in September' Hughes describes the Cranefly, with her face 'Like a pinhead dragon, with its tender moustache / And the simple colourless church window of her wings'. He shows us how to look deeper than we might otherwise look into the living treasure trove we have all but forgotten is ours. It is a wonderful gift, and one he passes on in poem after poem.

RAYMOND BRIGGS

'Tractor'

The tractor stands frozen – an agony
To think of. All night
Snow packed its open entrails. Now a head-pincering
    gale,
A spill of molten ice, smoking snow,
Pours into its steel.
At white heat of numbness it stands
In the aimed hosing of ground-level fieriness.

It defies flesh and won't start.
Hands are like wounds already
Inside armour gloves, and feet are unbelievable
As if the toe-nails were all just torn off.
I stare at it in hatred. Beyond it
The copse hisses – capitulates miserably
In the fleeing, failing light. Starlings,
A dirtier sleetier snow, blow smokily, unendingly, over
Towards plantations eastward.
All the time the tractor is sinking
Through the degrees, deepening
Into its hell of ice.

The starter lever
Cracks its action, like a snapping knuckle.
The battery is alive – but like a lamb

[73]

Trying to nudge its solid-frozen mother –
While the seat claims my buttock-bones, bites
With the space-cold of earth, which it has joined
In one solid lump.

I squirt commercial sure-fire
Down the black throat – it just coughs.
It ridicules me – a trap of iron stupidity
I've stepped into. I drive the battery
As if I were hammering and hammering
The frozen arrangement to pieces with a hammer
And it jabbers laughing pain-crying mockingly
Into happy life.

And stands
Shuddering itself full of heat, seeming to enlarge slowly
Like a demon demonstrating
A more-than-usually-complete materialization –
Suddenly it jerks from its solidarity
With the concrete, and lurches towards a stanchion
Bursting with superhuman well-being and abandon
Shouting Where Where?

Worse iron is waiting. Power-lift kneels,
Levers awake imprisoned deadweight,
Shackle-pins bedded in cast-iron cow-shit.
The blind and vibrating condemned obedience
Of iron to the cruelty of iron,
Wheels screeched out of their night-locks –

Fingers
Among the tormented
Tonnage and burning of iron

Eyes
Weeping in the wind of chloroform

And the tractor, streaming with sweat,
Raging and trembling and rejoicing.

Throughout this poem there is a wonderful interplay of opposites: cold becomes heat, bone becomes iron, the inanimate becomes animate. In the end, dead frozen iron becomes filled with joyous life.

Several of the other poems in *Moortown Diary* are about the care of farm animals and the anxiety and tension surrounding an animal giving birth. The idea of birth and animal suffering underlies the poem. On the surface, it is simply about getting an engine to start on a cold morning, but this commonplace event is used to express the elemental.

From the beginning the tractor is seen as an animal: 'entrails', 'head-pincering' (a birth image?) and 'numbness'. Amazingly, all the words used to describe extreme cold are those usually used to convey heat: 'molten, smoking, white heat, fieriness'. These are also associated with the furnaces where metal is made.

In the second verse, gloves, probably of leather, become 'armour', animal becomes metal. Then, in the painful image of the starting handle which 'cracks its action like a snapping knuckle', metal becomes animal. Even the battery inside the tractor is seen as a live creature (possibly still in the womb?) '. . . like a lamb trying to nudge its solid-frozen mother'. Buttock bones are so cold they become inanimate and at one with the iron seat, the earth itself and the coldness of outer space.

Tending the tractor, too, is like tending an animal:

> I squirt commercial sure-fire
> Down the black throat – it just coughs.

Eventually, when the tractor does come to life, it is almost like a birth. There is the same feeling of relief, success and joy. Something which was not fully alive, yet not actually dead, has burst into full life. It is like the moment of a newborn baby's first cry. The tractor leaps about:

> Bursting with superhuman well-being and abandon
> Shouting Where Where?

The tractor is not only alive, not only an animal, it is now almost human. It shouts and has a will of its own. From being a hated enemy it has been transformed into an eager comrade. In the final lines, the tractor becomes fully human:

> . . . streaming with sweat,
> Raging and trembling and rejoicing.

These lines also describe the physical state of the man struggling with the machine; at first raging, then trembling with effort and frustration and finally rejoicing. Man and machine have become one.

It has been said that the motor vehicle is the nearest the human race has come to creating a living thing. In this poem Ted Hughes makes the motor vehicle not only living, but part of life itself, at one with man and the earth, an elemental thing of hatred and joy, of death and birth.

I like this poem so much because it grows from an everyday, even banal, event which most of us have experienced: man versus machine . . . we can all empathize with Basil Fawlty when he lashes his car and screams at it. It is wonderful how Hughes takes such a pedestrian, potentially comic situation and transmutes it into something profound and deeply moving.

'New Year exhilaration'

On the third day
Finds its proper weather. Pressure
Climbing and the hard blue sky
Scoured by gales. The world's being
Swept clean. Twigs that can't cling
Go flying, last leaves ripped off
Bowl along roads like daring mice. Imagine
The new moon hightide sea under this
Rolling of air-weights. Exhilaration
Lashes everything. Windows flash,
White houses dazzle, fields glow red.
Seas pour in over the land, invisible maelstroms
Set the house-joints creaking. Every twig-end
Writes its circles, and the earth
Is massaged with roots. The powers of hills
Hold their bright faces in the wind-shine.
The hills are being honed. The river
Thunders like a factory, its weirs
Are tremendous engines. People
Walk precariously, the whole landscape
Is imperilled, like a tarpaulin
With the wind under it. 'It nearly
Blew me up the chymbley!' And a laugh
Blows away like a hat.

Over the years, Ted Hughes wrote enough classic poems to build a dry stonewall around Devon. They will weather beautifully. One particular favourite of mine is 'New Year exhilaration' from *Moortown Diary*, which shows the poet in Gerard Manley Hopkins mode (sans Dieu). Exhilaration is the key word, an ordinary day made extraordinary by the poet's vision, a poet in awe, and in love, with nature.

It is a poem that never fails to blow my hat off and make me smile.

LACHLAN MACKINNON

Moortown and River

___

In the early lines of 'Tintern Abbey', Wordsworth wrote of 'These hedgerows, hardly hedgerows, little lines / Of sportive wood run wild'. It is a characteristically Wordsworthian moment: the thing is not quite itself, but it is only a part of a great landscape passage in which all is subdued and homogenized in the manner of Claude. Wordsworth's imagination unifies, not only the scene, but the observer with the scene: something very different happens when, in 'Rain', Ted Hughes writes that 'The hedges / Are straggles of gap.' Here, the poet as diarist simply observes what is in front of him, leaving it to the landscape to show what if any unity it may have.

Moortown (1979), the sequence from which 'Rain' comes, has some of Hughes's freshest and liveliest writing. It is taken on the run, as though the poet feared that he might by rewriting undo his vision, like the snow in 'Roe-Deer' which is seen 'Revising its dawn inspiration / Back to the ordinary'. That it is diaristic does not mean it lacks mystery: the poet who 'Left to God the calf and his mother' in a storm knows of a sick calf that:

> The smell of the mown hay
> Mixed by moonlight with driftings of honeysuckle
> And dog-roses and foxgloves, and all
> The warmed spices of earth
> In the safe casket of stars and velvet

[79]

Did bring her to morning. And now she will live.

For all that one remembers the sequence primarily for its bleakness – ice, mud, blood and afterbirths – it can be not only tender, as here, but even joyful, when at harvest

> Like singing heard across evening water
> The tall loads are swaying towards their barns
> Down the deep lanes.

No other writer has given us a pastoral so emphatically earned.

Moortown seems to me an intensely masculine book, one in which the speaker stands outside a nature he must struggle to dominate. One might expect something similar from *River* (1983), a book mainly about fishing, but the voice here is quite other. First, it is more often retrospective from further ahead in time, as in 'Milesian Encounter on the Sligachan', recalling

> Only a little salmon.
> *Salmo salar*
> The loveliest, left-behind, most longed for ogress
> Of the Palaeolithic
> Watched me through her time-warped judas-hole
> In the ruinous castle of Skye
>
> As I faded from the light of reality.

Secondly, this voice often becomes possessed by what it experiences. In 'After Moonless Midnight', 'the whole river'

> Invisibly watched me. And held me deeper
> With its blind, invisible hands.
> 'We've got him,' it whispered, 'We've got him.'

The end of 'That Morning' finds the poet and his companion 'alive in the river of light / Among the creatures of light, creatures of light'.

And thirdly, this is a voice dedicated to a feminine principle, which in 'Torridge' is the river, 'She who has not once tasted death.' The characteristic imagery of this book is bridal and conjugal or erotic. In 'Low Water', 'the river is a beautiful idle woman':

> She lolls on her deep couch. And a long thigh
> Lifts from the flash of her silks.
>
> Adoring trees, kneeling, ogreish eunuchs
> Comb out her spread hair, massage her fingers.
>
> She stretches – and an ecstasy tightens
> Over her skin, and deep in her gold body
>
> Thrills spasm and dissolve. She drowses.

Hughes quickens an archaic reverence. Taken together, *Moortown* and *River* give us an account of man's dealings with the natural as full as Wordsworth's. Hughes makes his world so present that the things which would usually divide us from it seem mere 'straggles of gap'.

NICK GAMMAGE

'The Gulkana': Recognizing Home

Jumbled iceberg hills, away to the North –
And a long wreath of fire-haze.

The Gulkana, where it meets the Copper,
Swung, jade, out of the black spruce forest,
And disappeared into it.

Strange word, Gulkana. What does it mean?
A pre-Columbian glyph.
A pale blue thread – scrawled with a child's hand
Across our map. A Lazarus of water
Returning from seventy below.

We stumbled,

Not properly awake
In a weird light – a bombardment
Of purplish emptiness –
Among phrases that lumped out backwards. Among
    rocks
That kept startling me – too rock-like,
Hypnagogic rocks –

A scrapyard of boxy shacks
And supermarket refuse, dogs, wrecked pick-ups,
The Indian village where we bought our pass
Was comatose – on the stagnation toxins
Of a cultural vasectomy. They were relapsing

To Cloud-like-a-boulder, Mica, Bear, Magpie.

We hobbled along a tightrope shore of pebbles
Under a trickling bluff
That bounced the odd pebble onto us, eerily
(The whole land was in perpetual, seismic tremor.)
Gulkana –
Biblical, a deranging cry
From the wilderness – burst past us.
A stone voice that dragged at us.
I found myself clinging
To the lifted skyline fringe of rag spruce
And the subsidence under my bootsoles
With balancing glances – nearly a fear,
Something I kept trying to deny

With deliberate steps. But it came with me
As if it swayed on my pack –
A nape-of-the-neck unease. We'd sploshed far enough
Through the spongy sinks of the permafrost
For this river's
Miraculous fossils – creatures that each midsummer
Resurrected through it, in a blood-rich flesh.
Pilgrims for a fish!
Prospectors for the lode in a fish's eye!

In that mercury light, that ultra-violet,
My illusion developed. I felt hunted.
I tested my fear. It seemed to live in my neck –
A craven, bird-headed alertness.
And in my eye
That felt blind somehow to what I stared at
As if it stared at me. And in my ear –
So wary for the air-stir in the spruce-tips
My ear-drum almost ached. I explained it
To my quietly arguing, lucid panic
As my fear of one inside me,

A bodiless twin, some doppelgänger
Disinherited other, unliving,
Ever-living, a larva from prehistory,
Whose journey this was, who now exulted
Recognizing his home,
And whose gaze I could feel as he watched me
Fiddling with my gear – the interloper,
The fool he had always hated. We pitched our tent

And for three days
Our tackle scratched the windows of the express torrent.

We seemed underpowered. Whatever we hooked
Bent in air, a small porpoise,
Then went straight downriver under the weight
And joined the glacial landslide of the Copper
Which was the colour of cement.

Even when we got one ashore
It was too big to eat.

But there was the eye!
                    I peered into that lens
Seeking what I had come for. (What had I come for?
The camera-flash? The burned-out, ogling bulb?)
What I saw was small, crazed, snake-like.
It made me think of a dwarf, shrunken sun
And of the black, refrigerating pressures
Under the Bering Sea.

We relaunched their mulberry-dark torsos,
Those gulping, sooted mouths, the glassy visors –

Arks of an undelivered covenant,
Egg-sacs of their own Eden,
Seraphs of heavy ore

They surged away, magnetized,
Into the furnace boom of the Gulkana.

Bliss had fixed their eyes
Like an anaesthetic. They were possessed
By that voice in the river
And its accompaniment –
The flutes, the drumming. And they rose and sank
Like voices, themselves like singers
In its volume. We watched them, deepening away.
They looked like what they were, somnambulists,
Drugged, ritual victims, melting away
Towards a sacrament –
                       a consummation
That could only be death.
Which it would be, within some numbered days,
On some stony platform of water,
In a spillway, where a man could hardly stand –
Aboriginal Americans,
High among rains, in an opening of the hills,
They will begin to circle,
Shedding their ornaments,
In shufflings and shudders, male by female,
Begin to dance their deaths –
The current hosing over their brows and shoulders,
Bellies riven open and shaken empty
Into a gutter of pebbles
In the orgy of eggs and sperm,
The dance orgy of being reborn
From which masks and regalia drift empty,
Torn off – at last their very bodies,
In the numbed, languorous frenzy, as obstacles,
Ripped away –
                  ecstasy dissolving
In the mercy of water, at the star of the source,
Devoured by revelation,
Every molecule drained, and counted, and healed
Into the amethyst of emptiness -

I came back to myself. A spectre of fragments
Lifted my quivering coffee, in the aircraft,
And sipped at it.
I imagined the whole 747
As if a small boy held it
Making its noise. A spectre,
Escaping the film's flicker, peered from the porthole
Under the sun's colbalt core-darkness
Down at Greenland's corpse
Tight-sheeted with snow-glare.
                              Word by word
The voice of the river moved in me.
It was like lovesickness.
A numbness, a secret bleeding.
Waking in my body.
                    Telling of the King
Salmon's eye.
             Of the blood-mote mosquito.

And the stilt-legged, subarctic, one-rose rose
With its mock-aperture

Tilting towards us
In our tent-doorway, its needle tremor.

And the old Indian Headman, in his tatty jeans and
     socks, who smiled
Adjusting to our incomprehension – his face
A whole bat, that glistened and stirred.

The opening words of Ted Hughes's early and arguably best-
known poem 'The Thought-Fox' – 'I imagine' – have always
struck me as uncannily prophetic: the sanctity of the imagination, with its power to enrich experience and illuminate the inner
mythic world, has always been at the heart of his writing. 'The
Gulkana' is an eerie and astonishing example of the delicate
super-sensitive incisiveness of Hughes's poetic imagination. It is
the account of an arduous fishing expedition on a remote stretch

of a wild Alaskan river. But it is much more than that: through his poetic response to the pulse and music of this primeval world, and the fishermen's journey through it, he manages to evoke some elemental truth about his own nature and human nature more generally.

Towards the end of the poem, with delicate intimacy, he describes

> the stilt-legged, subarctic, one-rose rose
> With its mock aperture
> Tilting towards us
> In our tent-doorway, its needle tremor.

We feel that needle tremor oscillating throughout the poem as he takes spiritual bearings from the raw force and beauty of this elemental landscape and its fish, experienced with a sort of powerlessness. The shockwaves come as, trudging precariously along the shoreline with his son, he confronts the overwhelming power of the glacial river:

> Gulkana –
> Biblical, a deranging cry
> From the wilderness – burst past us.
> A stone voice that dragged at us.

The cumulative destructive effect of 'deranging', 'burst' and 'dragged' is terrifying. The river's unrestrained power threatens to dismantle the rational controls. Yet at the same time the energy feels liberating, a miracle of ecstasy. This surging, unforgiving environment unleashes something altogether different. Perhaps it is going too far – too provocatively – to suggest that Hughes celebrates the violence of this environment. But he surely *is* celebrating the release of an irrepressible, positive creative energy. He celebrates the holiness of that energy, which is the energy of his own creativeness. In his essay 'Poetry and Violence' he says:

The strong, positive mode of violence ought to concern us

more than the strong negative, since behind it presses the revelation of all that enables human beings to experience – with mystical clarity and certainty – what we call truth, reality, beauty, redemption and the kind of fundamental love that is at least equal to the fundamental evil.

It is as if he knows he is exposed to the massive force of Creation itself: the energy is energizing rather than threatening. There is something very characteristic about the water music in this poem; it is the eerie Bacchanalian music of flutes and drums which is the beat of ecstatic celebration. Music and water are two of the great liberators in Ted Hughes's poems, returned to for their liberating spontaneity. The energy is reminiscent of the positive life force of Blake's *The Marriage of Heaven and Hell* and those pivotal soliloquies in Shakespeare. It recalls that moment in Hughes's 1971 interview with Ekbert Faas in which he observes that the energy, if uncontrolled through ritual, can destroy you.

Hughes conjures this conflict with uncanny clarity, as if his whole life has been a series of skirmishes on the frontline. In the fishermen's perilous journey he senses the tension between the rational, analytical part of our nature (what he has called 'objective intelligence') and the spontaneous-instinctive side (in his words, the 'inner world, of natural impulsive response'). The sense in the poem is that these have got unhealthily out of balance. Something precious has been lost in the process; the fishermen feel 'underpowered' as they try to land the massive King Salmon, the Chinook (Hughes reckons some of those that got away weighed up to 60 lb).

This tension is the revelation at the heart of the poem. It comes to him, treading gingerly along that pebbly shoreline. He feels it as a fear, a 'nape-of-the-neck unease'. He feels challenged, placed in the dock. He experiences the fear as

> my fear of one inside me,
> A bodiless twin, some doppelgänger
> Disinherited other, unliving,

Ever-living, a larva from prehistory,
Whose journey this was, who now exulted
Recognizing his home

He feels this psychic misalignment, too, in the way 'civilization' has reduced the Indian settlement where he buys his fishing pass, robbing it of its spiritual richness. He describes with despair the village with its 'supermarket refuse' and 'wrecked pick-ups' which was 'comatose' on 'the stagnation toxins / Of a cultural vasectomy'. The journey of the huge King Salmon comes as a sharp contrast to that of the fishermen. There is no self-doubt or hesitation in their surging drive upriver, heading for the breeding grounds. Theirs is like the ruthless journey of the sperm (partly why that image of a 'cultural vasectomy' had such resonance). It is a fearless journey to the limits (death), which brings life: rebirth through the redeeming power of water.

The geography of this conflict is very similar to that of the mythic journey in Joseph Conrad's *Heart of Darkness* in which Marlow, on deck in the 'brooding gloom', recalls a journey into the raw heart of things through a similarly untamed wilderness, becoming exposed to civilizing pressure. And, as in Marlow's yarn, it is the purity of the wilderness which is so haunting. Hughes responds spiritually to its elemental, unpredictable and untamed beauty. Powerful analogies for this wild landscape abound in Ted Hughes's work. One of the most striking is the character of Jocasta as he created her in his version of Seneca's *Oedipus* for Peter Brook. He developed Jocasta from an insignificant minor backdrop in the Seneca to the smouldering core of his own version. Hughes's Jocasta is like this wild Alaskan water scape, all elemental muscularity and drive. She challenges Oedipus's hesitant rationality as the river and its fish challenge Hughes's. As with Jocasta's big speeches in Hughes's *Oedipus*, 'The Gulkana' is driven by the potency and sensuousness of its physical life: the rush of the torrent, the strain of the massive hooked fish bending in the air, the precarious walk along the shoreline. The poem draws you in with its intimacy and minutely

observed detail. Hughes's storytelling gift is formidable: hypnotic, mythic, and intimate. He is sharing something crucial.

The relentlessness with which Hughes pursued this spiritual
conflict leaps up from the drafts of this poem, held at Emory
University in Georgia – all 150 pages of them. Reading them is
like watching a sculptor break through into his material to find
the life inside: Bernini reaching into the marble for his St Theresa.
Perhaps the intensity of the re-drafting is itself the evidence of a
further skirmish in the battle between the rational and the
instinctive.

This tension in Hughes's work between the two polarized
aspects of our nature is everywhere: in those Crow songs, for
example, and the two conflicting versions of Reverend Lumb in
Gaudete. But nowhere is it faced more courageously, I think,
than in 'The Gulkana'. The urgency comes through because
Hughes feels naturally drawn to this environment, linked by an
umbilical cord. He feels intimate with its beauty, power and
threats. It has the wild foreboding starkness of his childhood
landscapes. Seeing the Gulkana, Hughes recognizes his home:
just as (and he made this explicit in the early drafts of the poem)
he had dreamed he would. 'The Gulkana' has the aura of
mystical revelation.

What is it that makes Hughes's poetry here – his characteristic
voice – so haunting and vivid? It is clearly a complex mystery.
But one part of his special gift is the tender and delicate vividness
of his description: the manifestation of his ability to see,
experience and conjure with such magical clarity. The delicacy
and penetrative detail – his way of seeing – is almost miraculous.
His description of the salmon, for example:

> We relaunched their mulberry-dark torsos,
> Those gulping, sooted mouths, the glassy visors – . . .

> They surged away, magnetized,
> Into the furnace boom of the Gulkana.

Simply trying to see and hear in this way, to emulate the technique, feels physically difficult. So where does the gift come from? Perhaps there is a clue in something Ted Hughes once wrote about two of his most admired poets who so obviously share this gift – Shakespeare and John Clare. Clare's gift, he thought, has something to do with a special kind of love:

> As a love-poet – horrible term – a poet who is able to love in some total, unconditional way, and to set his feelings in verse unself-consciously, he is the only one in our whole tradition, to my mind, who resembles Shakespeare.

Shakespeare, too, has things to say about the idea that this special love – something we could tritely call a love of all living things – can empower the senses to see and experience with an extra incision and intuition. It is there in *Love's Labour's Lost*, when Berowne says that love

> with the motion of all elements,
> Courses as swift as thought in every power,
> And gives to every power a double power,
> Above their functions and their offices.
> It adds a precious seeing to the eye;
> A lover's eyes will gaze an eagle blind;
> A lover's ear will hear the lowest sound,
> When the suspicious head of theft is stopped:
> Love's feeling is more soft and sensible
> Than are the tender horns of cockled snailes:
> Love's tongue proves dainty Bacchus gross in taste.

Whatever the root of Hughes's gift, it ignites in his writing something valuable and rare.

MEDBH MCGUCKIAN

Moortimes

After Moortown

Those lilies, ghosts of white wines unsipped,
I gave them back to the soil
and watched your mind disappear
down some avenue of trees
where Wordsworth beat his head or Yeats wrapped
   his arms.

What do you sip, I wonder,
at this eleventh hour,
staring at the impossible book?
I'll pretend Shelley lives in you
as the golden fire in your eyes,
half-peasant in its origin,
makes me settle near you,
tests my ideal like a new ladies' nib.

I'll be the ghost of your blue spare room,
I'll go on consulting you,
holding your arm bare to feel
the French skin that listens
as a woman only listens.

To go alone to the alone
is to see a secret afternoon of poetry

darting past me in a doorway
to the end of the terrace
in the untrue rain.

Yet you said that the hand when alone
is bent into a potent amulet in itself,
and the middle of the week
would go so quickly
if the weather took it into
its head to clear up.

It cost you nothing, it was one
of your possessions, on your grass
the same butterfly is glued to the same
sunflower, with no excitement greater
than bees swarming until next winter.

Whilst I in my marsh tell you nakedly,
there are bees everywhere but where
they should be, though their honey
still graces our breakfasts
with minute perforations of toothmarks.

I am afraid in the promised week
the river will be too full,
and I'll outtalk those birds again,
or hate the marble mantlepiece
for making my face so smooth.

This building in its infancy
substituted vessel for breast, old-fashioned
being words of praise. October's betrayal
the loose-coated painter dwelling on uncleanness.
All their washing will not make you inherit
my gondola character, little breast,
little mother, clapping your crushed hands.

'After Moortown' is unpublished until now although it was in
fact written expressly for Ted Hughes in the early 1980s when I

was an apprentice-journeywoman in his trade. If it seems half-asleep and inchoate in its self-taughtness it's also because at the time I was still recuperating very gradually from what I believe partly killed Sylvia Plath, the trauma of 'giving' birth and its aftermath. Hughes's own collection *Moortown* spoke to me then with a cogent comfort. It was probably one of the few texts I could at all relate to in that groping, the only one I could or did find written by an intelligence that encompassed or came anywhere near confronting the harrowing, soul-splitting, body-shattering experience I had barely emerged from. I never sent it to him or indeed to *anyone*, but it was a release and thank-you for the gift of his own stark and brutal farm-poems, where he provided a vehicle for the unsayable and what has to be forgotten.

I have never come across a poetic equivalent by a woman poet who has become a mother on the immensity, the gravity, of childbirth. Certainly I myself was not equal to it, the volcanic in the virgin Dickinson. *Moortown* came closest to the raw shock that was indescribable, the human courage to express so honestly the intimately rippable connectors and filaments between all animal sexuality, and the beginning and end moment of our lives. I felt Hughes showed there despite or through his own devastation how pain only seems to dominate those thresholds. It was of course the bleak pessimism that my depression responded to, but with such a positive influence that I was able to partially surmount it and choose him then as Muse, albeit English and male, in the last months of my defiant second pregnancy, when my fear of a renewed possession by demons was at its height.

So the ink here has very much dried, I'm afraid, and the lilies that were for my first book and on its cover, long since festered. That child Hugh is doing his O-levels and it turned out an O-level of a birth.

Now in the tremulous turn of the years it is the beautiful 1983 edition of *River* with its concurrent photographs that I am most elated by, that I found too ironic *then* in my own Moortime. I am writing this now in Limerick looking out at the Shannon below Lough Derg, and reading John Mitchel's *Jail Journal* in the antipodes:

> Visit from Terence MacManus; he has ridden up the valley of the Derwent and Clyde from New Norfolk, to see us by stealth ... we have ridden about twelve miles north-west from Bothwell, to see the Shannon ... a rushing, whirling tumultuous stream that derives its waters from the 'Big Lake', a noble reservoir some thirty miles further to the northwest, lying high on a desolate plateau of Tasmania ... Through the whole of its course this river runs very rapidly, having a fall of two thousand feet in those thirty miles; and like all the other Van Diemen's Land rivers, it is icy cold.
>
> All my life long I have delighted in rivers, rivulets, rills, fierce torrents tearing their rocky beds, gliding dimpled brooks kissing a daisied marge. The rumble, or murmur, or deep-resounding roll, or raving roar of running water is of all sounds my ears ever hear now the most homely. Nothing else in this land looks or sounds like home ...
>
> I delight in poets who delight in rivers; and for this do I love that sweet singer, through whose inner ear and brain the gush of his native Aufidus for ever streamed and flashed ... But, hold – plump into the water, just under the bank, tumbles a *Platypus* ...

I love the way in *River* the English and Irish rivers confluesce with the Welsh and Scottish ones, so you are able to appreciate them as Wordsworth would have wanted. Through the themes of healing and restoration through the renewals of love, Seamus Heaney flows too, in some phrases that hold their kinship – the last line 'And mind condenses on old haws' could be the first line of *The Haw Lantern*. Because the single occasion where I heard Hughes read was in Derry, two days after my father died, I think of him, I am sure falsely, as he appeared then in my Moortime of death, mediated to me by Heaney, a brooding moon with a protective sun. Those *River* poems, Elizabethan in their perfection, state even more clearly the unspeakable about 'The Facts of Life' but use a spiritual language as carefully as a priest wipes cruets or chalice at the Lavabo:

> a cry, half sky, half bird,
> slithered over roots

In 'Low Water' Hughes captures a mood or state of female auto-arousal few women poets have equalled, with the simple earthiness of Gauguin. His 'Eel' poem, soft as Marianne Moore, loving as Elizabeth Bishop, draws us in to contemplate the 'Damascened' identity of 'the nun of water'. In 'Last Night' the river is dying less from pollution than because he is wading there; in 'River' it is Christ being baptized. 'That Morning' rhyming 'solemn' with 'salmon' and 'imperishable' with 'fish', consoles after the energy of 'Night Arrival of Sea-Trout' where to say 'Honeysuckle hanging her fangs' is to repopulate a jungle. 'Stump Pool in April' is like Chagall, 'Dee' relates the male-child-river to the holding, waiting landscape. While 'New Year' continues with *Moortown* Caesarian imagery, the amazing opening poem explores creation itself, climaxing in the thought-fox again.

Rita Ann Higgins's review of *Birthday Letters* in *Poetry Ireland* (Autumn 1998) crystallizes the cautious mix of prejudice, scepticism, reserve and respect with which we women poets have split our loyalty between Plath and her gifted survivor. To step back into Sylvia's shoes, with Nuala ní Dhomnáill's permission, I conclude with my translation of her 'An Prionsa Dubh', a lightish-hearted *Bell-Jar* accepting total responsibility for the sins of the daughter. I was once very kindly sent a copy of *Lupercal* signed to me by Ted at 'The Bull Moses' with 'To Medbh of the Bulls'. So to 'The Bull Ted', Ted of the 'raptures and rendings', I offer this.

The Ebony Adonis

At puberty I had a dream
in my all-too-single bunk in the school dorm
of dancing the length of a public room
with the guts of my relatives looking on
in the arms of an ebony Adonis.

Round and round whirled the waltz
till my senses spun with joy
from the fiery, fierce glance of his eye.
Every achievement in fitness and sport
possessed my ebony Adonis.

The dormitory door caved in with a bang,
lights snapped on and wash-basins rang,
a well-fed sister was singing the praises of Christ,
and myself left amidst the bedclothes bereft
of my ebony Adonis.

His face and his touch I will never forget,
that high-powered shadow that with me slept,
that expert lover that spoiled me for dead,
my sovereign, imperial, absolute passion,
my ebony Adonis.

My daughter in her turn dreamed aged nine
of a door that led to a spellbound inn
where various chancers were coaxing her in,
and like mother, like daughter, you'd know she was mine,
nothing would do her but the ebony Adonis.

Now light of my soul, make no bones about it,
a no-good son of a bitch can't be trusted,
with his murder record and black belt too,
this Lord of the Dance is headed, where to?
Straight through the fires of hell, with the ebony Adonis.

You'll end up closed in an exhibition case,
under lock and key, or caught as it were in a revolving
   doorway
unable to either get in or out for the swish
back and forth night and day through the porches of
   the psyche
if you give an inch to the ebony Adonis.

You'll be laid low as I was in a type of M.E.,
at the dregs of a well like a sort of Ophelia,
tortured with symptoms for fourteen years,
without a creature to speak to or a sympathetic ear
since I handed my cards to the ebony Adonis.

Till I walked out over the golf links to the moonless tide
and summoned up the Goddess and the spirits of my tribe
to gather around me, and swore my solemn promise
to surrender what I loved most to exorcise the sickness –
all very well for a joke, except this was my ebony Adonis.

Who was all along Sir Death, lurking in ambush
in my womb's valleys, in the summer-house
and lowlands of my heart, forever alert
to decoy me into his desert, to destroy me in short,
being the ebony Adonis sort.

Still my honeychild, since I've been there and done it,
you do your own thing and don't give a shit,
for Old Death will not get us, though he'll not let us go
any more than this life will condone us one kiss
from our ebony Adonis.

Nuala ní Dhomnáill
Translated from the Irish by Medbh McGuckian.

'The black day splits with lightning'

Prometheus on his Crag is the first book by Ted Hughes which I ever bought. I ordered it in response to the first letter I ever got from Olwyn Hughes. I had written to Keith Gordon about the Rainbow Press in June 1973. I got a letter from Olwyn on 11 June indicating that Keith Gordon was no longer with them. She went on to note that although a new book, *Prometheus on his Crag*, 'won't be published until next month, all copies are now sold except two, and I am provisionally reserving one of these for you for a couple weeks until I hear from you. Do let me know quickly if you want one. It's going to be a splendid little book, rather like *Eat Crow* but with more interesting contents I feel, and the drawing by Leonard Baskin is quite splendid.'

I ordered it on 14 June for $50.

There were delays. I didn't get the book until December. But it was worth the wait. Once I had read it – over and over – I determined to read everything that I could find by Hughes and may even have started becoming a Hughes collector at the time; though, as Terry Belanger says, you aren't a true collector until you order *two* copies of a new work and it wasn't until *Orts* was published in 1978 that I did that.

Prometheus on his Crag is a series of twenty-one poems about a prisoner. While the protagonist is called Prometheus, this is not the Prometheus of Aeschylus with his foreknowledge which potentially gives leverage with his captor, or the Trickster

Prometheus of Hesiod who seemed almost compelled to keep pushing the envelope with just one trick too many, and it is certainly not the proud, defiant, revolutionary Prometheus of Shelley or Marx, no matter how much these may resonate in it. Instead, as Hughes pointed out, this is 'a numb poem about numbness'; this a new Prometheus. A twentieth-century Prometheus. An existential Prometheus from the 'limbo' of the *univers concentrationnaire*. This is a Prometheus with angst and dread, condemned to freedom.

There are numerous well documented cases of prisoners having sudden astonishing transformations. Mihajlo Mihajlov alone cited dozens of examples in his 'Mystical Experiences in Soviet Labour Camps', and (this was 1973) Solzhenitsyn had just introduced the word 'gulag' into English as a common noun (not an acronym). Yet what was written about *Prometheus on his Crag* – informed criticism one would assume since, as Keith Sagar and Stephen Tabor note, there were only 'slightly over 160 copies printed' – focused on that abrupt shift in poem twenty-one. Ekbert Faas referred to the 'rather artificially tagged on last poem'. Schofield felt the 'image of an integrated psyche comes perhaps too abruptly', 'too suddenly'. And Sweeting described it as 'a beautiful but unconvincingly precipitate release'.

It is that 'precipitate release' which seems to come 'too abruptly', 'too suddenly', which was, I feel, the very effect that Hughes was consciously aiming for. The reason that the printing of the book had been delayed until November was that Hughes had radically changed poem twenty-one after the final proofs (these revised proofs are contained in the extensive Hughes archive acquired by Emory University in Atlanta, and available to scholars). Right up to the last minute he was concerned with getting it exactly right. Every line was changed. It was changed from what was essentially the subjunctive mood to the indicative – like the difference between 'fiat lux' and 'erat lux' – so that it was no longer performative, it was constative. The original allowed for agency – the captor? Prometheus himself? the mother? – it implied volition. The final version emphasizes Hughes's intent to demonstrate the inexplicable nature of the 'release'. It just happens.

Later the commercial publication of the Prometheus poems in *Moortown* (1979) would confirm that Hughes felt the abrupt change in the final poem was the effect he sought. That twenty-first poem remains the same while three of the others have been deleted and replaced by completely new poems. Critics could now dismiss the whole series as transitional or, as Gifford and Roberts noted, perhaps indicative too of a hiatus in the development of Hughes's poetry following the completion or abandonment of *Crow*.

The 'sudden' liberation of a captive seems to reside outside of the parameters of the Prometheus legend or literature of the quest of the Orghast experiment, or even Hughes's own private mythology. Perhaps the origins may be found more simply, in the literal experience of an actual prisoner. Hughes, along with Daniel Weissbort, had become co-editor of the new publication, *Modern Poetry in Translation*, in 1965 and continued in that role for the first ten issues. During that time the journal printed work by poets from all over the world but the ones that Hughes seems to have found the most congenial were those from Eastern Europe, particularly Herbert, Popa, Holub and Pilinszky. There seems to have been a special bond between Hughes and Janos Pilinszky. By 1973 Hughes had known Pilinszky for years. He had translated three of Pilinszky's poems for the seventh issue of *Modern Poetry in Translation* in 1970 – a year before the first Prometheus poem appeared in a periodical (*Workshop*, September 1971) – and he would later publish a selection of Pilinszky's work. Indicative of their close relationship is, for example, Pilinszky's dedication of a poem ('Unfinished Past') to Hughes. For his part, Hughes seemed fascinated by Pilinszky; besides their extensive correspondence at the Emory Archive there is one whole box – number 27 – of Pilinszky material with a label from Hughes's own inventory: 'A mass of material (6" thick) very curious to me.' The epiphany that Pilinszky experienced in the camps at the end of World War II has been described by Hughes:

'the world of the camps became the world of his deepest, most private, poetic knowledge'. Hughes poses the question: 'how is it, we might well ask, that this vision of what is, after all, a Universe of Death, an immovable, an unalterable horror, where trembling creatures still go uselessly through their motions, how is it that it issues in poems so beautiful and satisfying?'

As elsewhere Hughes, in describing someone else's work, is able to shed light on his own achievement. Another resonance for Prometheus can be found in Hughes's verdict on Pilinszky: 'the moment closest to extinction turns out to be *the* creative moment.'

SIMON ARMITAGE

Discovering *Gaudete*

I first read *Gaudete* when I was twenty. I was at college, studying geography for some unknown reason, but at the same time making my way along the library's contemporary poetry shelf. I think I was homesick for West Yorkshire, and reckoned that by reading Hughes I might be able to keep in touch.

Every now and again you're taken in by a book the way that sleep sometimes happens – unexpectedly, thinking maybe you'll just cat-nap for ten minutes, then wake up in a different part of the day, the world having moved on. I was down in a basement, in the laundry room, killing an hour and a half while an industrial-size washer clicked and rumbled its way through its cycle and the big empty dryers breathed warm air into the room. There was nobody else around.

Gaudete begins with an outline of the story to come, in which Hughes describes the abduction of Anglican clergyman Nicholas Lumb by spirits from the other world. Lumb is needed for some unspecified task, and to fill his place in the everyday world the spirits create a double from an oak log, whose job it is to go on ministering the gospel of love during the vicar's absence. As it turns out, the changeling goes at his task quite literally, organizing a coven amongst the women, in which seduction and sex is a form of initiation. Not surprisingly, the husbands, brothers and fathers of the parish are less keen on this interpretation of the Bible, and eventually rise up against the doppelgänger to kill him. In the epilogue the original Lumb returns, and wanders the West of Ireland composing strange poems to a female goddess.

That introduction reads very much like a treatment or proposal for a film, and in fact the book was written with that in mind. But it becomes clear in the first few pages that what Hughes has put together has a life very much of its own, without any need of translation into another art form. For one thing, *Gaudete* is written in a style that dances around somewhere on the border between poetry and prose; lines of unequal length, present-tense stage directions that propel the storyline but at the same time identify the finest of details, in terms of emotion as well as image. Lumb's disappearance begins with the familiar nightmare scenario of becoming lost in half-remembered streets. Hughes describes the place where Lumb finds himself:

> Heavy cattle are surging through the gangways
> Driven through banging steel gates
> By bellowing men
> Who jab them with electrified clubs.
> The white bull hangs from a winch
> Like a cat swung up by the scruff of its neck.
> Lumb is spreadeagled beneath it.
> A long-handled hook rips the bull's underbelly from
>   ribs to testicles.

After Lumb's blood-bath in the guts of the bull suspended above him – a kind of reverse baptism – it becomes clear that this isn't going to be quite the fairy story that the introduction predicted, and Hughes has never been one for dodging the more gory aspects of this life or any other. Nevertheless, *Gaudete* creates its own context for this, offsetting scenes of furious violence against moments of fantastic delicacy, such as the two-and-a-bit-page description of Mrs Holroyd sunbathing in the garden while nothing happens, or Mrs Westlake, hypnotized by her own thoughts, hearing 'her watch whispering, listening to it, as if trapped inside it'. The book isn't without its comic possibilities either, as when Mrs Garten entertains the lookalike Lumb in the garden hut, with rabbits and ferrets spilling out of their cages around the heaving bodies.

What's so powerful about *Gaudete* is its passion – that sensation, as if a line is writing itself in front of your own eyes, which I'm sure is related to a feeling the author might have experienced during the creation of the line itself. There's also a way in which the book delivers far more than it promises; a screenwriter might be content with constructing images designed to work on the retina, but Hughes's words on the page travel right through the optic nerve, discharging something infinitely more profound.

When I'd finished reading, the washing machine had stopped spinning, and I was sat in complete silence under a single light bulb in the small hours of the morning, the possessor of a new knowledge. I kept the book, which was wrong, but cost me a four quid fine, and in any event I somehow felt I'd earned it, as if ownership of the book certificated the experience of reading it. I tend to believe that all good books consume the circumstances and surroundings of the reader, and I still can't think of a tumble dryer without the Rev. Nicholas Lumb coming to mind, even though (as far as I'm aware) there's no meaningful connection.

(This article first appeared in the *Sunday Times*.)

FAY GODWIN

Ted Hughes and *Elmet*

Ted Hughes originally suggested that I take pictures in the Calder Valley in 1970, after an unexpectedly hilarious portrait session just before publication of *Crow*. He liked the portraits, and asked if I ever did landscape photographs. I responded that I did walk a great deal and sometimes carried a camera. He told me there was an area in the Calder Valley which he wanted to write about, but felt the need for a visual 'trigger'. I was ready for such a project, and got on with it, but did not hear from Ted again until 1976, when I had just been diagnosed as having 'terminal' cancer. Ted told me to 'turn the current positive' and get on with the book. I already had some pictures and he had some of the poems. He was totally generous and supportive. And we worked on the book through 1977.

The result was *Remains of Elmet* in 1979. After about 45,000 copies had been sold the printers went out of business, the origination material was lost and the book went out of print. In 1994, in spite of Faber's great reluctance, because of the cost of reproducing the photographs, a completely new edition called *Elmet* was published, with about one-third new pictures and poems, much better designed and produced. It won design and production awards but was hardly publicized, and even dropped off the British Books in Print listing. The last communication I had from Ted was in March 1998 when he wrote of *Elmet*: 'that's our classic so we'll keep it in print.' I hope his wish is honoured.

Ted was never patronizing, which would have been so easy. I believe the work flourished because of the open and reciprocal nature of the working relationship. We wanted the work to be complementary, obliquely equivalent. We were determined not to 'illustrate' each other's work: for example, in one poem he felt that he had described my picture too literally, and wanted to drop the poem. I liked the poem, so I took a new picture to distance it somewhat, and that turned out to be a far better picture anyway. Obviously there was a more fundamental dissatisfaction with the poem, since Ted dropped it in the later 1994 version, whereas my photograph remained, in a different context. He repeated, on a number of occasions, that this was his definitive collection of Calder Valley poems.

I had not known about Ted's illness, so his death was a shock and a deep sorrow. I was looking forward to showing him a small colour book which I am self-publishing, since we had corresponded on the subject of colour photography. I shall miss those letters with the strong and rhythmic script. He was my contemporary, a strong reference point in my life, a source of generosity and inspiration, and I still cannot believe that he has been felled.

Portrait of Ted Hughes by Fay Godwin, 1970

ANTHONY THWAITE
Yorkshire and *Elmet*

———

Ted Hughes was born in August 1930 in Mytholmroyd (between Hebden Bridge and Halifax) in what was then the West Riding of Yorkshire. In his broadcast essay 'The Rock', he described Scout Rock, the place that dominated his early boyhood horizon. At the age of eight he moved with his family to Mexborough, to the south-east of that Riding: colliery country, rather than a landscape of the decaying textile mills. Even when he left Mexborough Grammar School at the age of eighteen to do his national service in the RAF, he spent most of that service on a posting in Yorkshire.

I was born in June 1930. By what I think of as an accident of timing, I was born in Chester: my father's employment in Lloyds Bank meant that he was moved from one place to another every few years, and at the time of my birth he was a cashier in the Chester branch. But in 1933 we moved to Leeds, then in 1938 to Sheffield; both of them large industrial cities in the West Riding.

So Ted and I shared a Yorkshire childhood. More importantly, as far as I'm concerned, I was brought up to have a strong sense of belief that I was ancestrally completely Yorkshire. My father's father, Simon, came from a long line of tenant farmers – stretching back unbroken to the seventeenth century, and, with plenty of genealogical evidence, long before that – in the North Riding of Yorkshire, in Wensleydale and Swaledale. 'The Dales' were full of cousins and cousins' cousins. They were our prolific kin, and our holidays in the 1930s were almost entirely spent in the Dales. My mother's side – Mallinsons, Handforths – was almost entirely West Riding: Bradford, Halifax, Brighouse.

Ted's sequence of poems *Remains of Elmet* (1979), with its haunting photographs by Fay Godwin, is sub-titled 'A Pennine Sequence'. In a prefatory note, he wrote:

> The Calder Valley, west of Halifax, was the last ditch of Elmet, the last British Celtic kingdom to fall to the Angles. For centuries it was considered a more or less uninhabitable wilderness, a notorious refuge for criminals, a hide-out for refugees. Then in the early 1800s it became the cradle for the Industrial Revolution in textiles, and the upper Calder became the 'hardest-worked river in England'.
>
> Throughout my lifetime, since 1930, I have watched the mills of the region and their attendant chapels die. Within the last fifteen years the end has come. They are now virtually dead, and the population of the valley and the hillsides, so rooted for so long, is changing rapidly.

I knew something of this in my childhood (I was keen on the past, and on what I came to know as 'archaeology', from an early age). In 1953, when I was a young adult, my parents moved to what was to be their last house together, in Scarcroft, between Leeds and Wetherby: I knew that this was part of the 'kingdom', with Barwick in Elmet just down the road and Sherburn in Elmet a bit further east.

Though I suppose it *might* have been possible, with all my historical and archaeological passions, for me to have made some use of this, I have never done so. Without knowing Hughes's genealogical tree, I somehow have the notion that he attached as much importance to his strands of Welsh ancestry (the Hughes part) as he did to the Yorkshire blood. So the embattled 'last British Celtic kingdom' produced a fruitful clash of genes as well as images of industrial energy and post-industrial, post-Christian decay. I envy him that. Certainly *Remains of Elmet* is a Hughes work which I praise with unqualified admiration.

My name, 'Thwaite', is not part of Angle etymology but Norse: *thveit* is Old Norse for 'a clearing in a wood'. It's a place name as well as a family name, of course, found on its own as well as in compounds (Applethwaite, Seathwaite, etc.) in Cumbria, North Yorkshire (there's a hamlet at the top of Swaledale called Thwaite), and in East Anglia: within thirty or so miles of where I have lived for the past twenty-five years in Norfolk there are three villages, north and south, called Thwaite. So those Norsemen, in the intervals of burning, pillaging and looting, presumably settled. And they are my ancestors.

Ted plays marvellously with such roots and delvings in his poem 'Thistles':

> Every one a revengeful burst
> Of resurrection, a grasped fistful
> Of splintered weapons and Icelandic frost thrust up
>
> From the underground stain of a decayed Viking.
> They are like pale hair and the gutturals of dialect.
> Every one manages a plume of blood.

So, from 'a decayed Viking' to a Celtic Yorkshireman, or a Yorkshire Celt, thanks.

A Measure of Grace: The Teacher's Story

Inevitably, I brought all my teacherly preoccupations to my reading of *What is the Truth*? This 'Farmyard Fable for the Young' excited me with its huge potential for the classroom. It would delight and, at the same time, empower children to reflect on their own writing within the secure framework of story and poetry.

The sequence of poems is linked by a prose fable theme. God's Son begs to visit Earth. There he believes he will discover the 'Truth' of the creatures the people know best. Reluctantly, God leads his Son to a hillside and summons the sleeping villagers:

> In their sleep they will say what they truly know. When they are awake, they are deepest asleep. When they are asleep, they are widest awake.

In the dream state these people coin surreal imagery which sometimes shifts through powerful metamorphoses but is always committed to return them to reality with senses more sharply attuned to earth.

And so each villager is put under test to speak the 'Truth' of a chosen creature. The moment is critical, the Truth elusive, the judgement uncompromising. Sometimes, however, ultimate reality is almost addressed in images which combine so potently that excitement stirs on the hillside:

of the foal:

> Suddenly he's here – a warm heap
> Of ashes and embers, fondled by small draughts.

Of the hare:

> The hare is a very fragile thing,
> the life in the hare is a glassy goblet and her yellow-fringed
> > Frost-flake belly says: Fragile.

The voices are richly diverse and a leavening of humour expressed in cheerful, lighthearted 'naming' is as integral to the whole as the beauty of the more lyrical pieces. For instance, the poacher's rat ends:

> Bobby-robin, knacker-knocker
> Sneak-knicker, sprinty-dinty
> Pintle-bum

And appropriately enough the Son asks, 'Was that everything but the Truth?' Then there is the farmer's jaundiced view of cows:

> Nothing can stop
> From one end the Moo
> From t'other the flop
> > flop
> > flop
> > flipperty-flop
> Flopperty-flipperty

– a view resolved so beautifully in his daughter's lyrical response:

> And there's a ruined holy city
> In a herd of lying down, cud-chewing cows –
> Noses raised, eyes nearly closed
> They are fragments of temples –

The balance is redressed and God, quite properly, is better

pleased. It was, however, the farmer who, predictably, provided the image relished most by my own pupils:

> A cowclap is an honest job,
> A black meringue for the flies.

There is both delight and tension in the precarious balance of these varied voices. At any moment, scatology flows into lyricism, the sacred into the profane. Perhaps most importantly, these poems are acutely humane, the creatures projections of ourselves, the villagers vulnerable to mood and circumstance as they are thrown painfully on their own reserves of wit and courage.

Always, however, God's judgement underlines the ultimate futility of the task. This divine dissatisfaction is the necessary frustration of the poet whose destiny is to strive endlessly to emulate the first great act of creation when the creatures were named and came into being. And yet, throughout, there is a driving sense of possibility within endless permutations of words. Moreover, each poem is spoken – and this is an act of celebration. The villagers listen and react within the tight circle of their wholehearted intention. And always there is the tension of knowing that ultimately the onus is on God to answer his own question:

> 'The Truth,' said God finally, 'is this. The Truth is that I was that Fox. Just as I was that Foal I am each of these things. The Rat. The Fly. And each of these things is Me. It is. It is. That is the Truth.'

This stark response dissatisfies our human ear. We mortals prefer Ted Hughes's poems which grant us some dim, intuitive sense of the infinite, just a hint of immortality. Significantly, almost every page glows with an illustrative moon, a pale light which suffuses the earthbound coupling worms as surely as the flight of the swallow. It is a mark of the divine within creation, what Ted Hughes called 'the holiness of existence'. At the very end the Father returns to heaven. The Son, however, remains on earth, bound to struggling humanity. In the distance the cocks begin to crow, and our culture insists they crow for betrayal as well as for the dawn.

Children engage readily in the mental role play which casts them as villagers tested by God. Their youthful audacity is their faith in the oneness of the community of writers. They too must aspire to the impossible. And not only must they write, but, like the villagers, they must speak their poems with passion and subtlety. It is the physicality of the word which, at once, roots it to earth and aspires to sublimity. This was particularly evident at an Observer Children's Poetry award ceremony where one of my pupils spoke the following poem in the presence of the Poet Laureate. Politely declining the offer of a microphone, twelve-year-old Adam filled the hall with his voice and created a moment both tribal and celebratory. Hughes smiled quietly, apparently pondering the mystery that makes the writer, and, most importantly, warmed by this evidence of the word renewed in the next generation.

The Goldfish . . .

Is a splinter of mineral,
mined by Neptune.
Nothing stirs
in its own narrow world of undisturbed peace.

Its comfort . . .
Reflection.
The duel begins –
a quick bolt from watching eyes
from above,
a challenge with no end.

The goldfish is a sort of . . .
Delicate feather
made from tiny mirrors,
reflecting everything beautiful.

Its eyes look like frog-spawn
with minute tadpoles in the middle.

I feed it. I clean it. And talk to it.
But I get nothing in return . . .
As if its body is here,
yet its mind is in a coma far, far away.
I wonder if it can hear me.
I get nothing in return
from this delicate splinter of a fish.

Adam Hughes (12 years)

But the question remains: why does *What is the Truth?* work such peculiar magic in an ordinary classroom? Ted Hughes's own words provide a clue. In a letter to Lissa Paul, quoted in her essay 'Inside the Lurking-glass with Ted Hughes', he writes about finding 'a lingua franca – a style of communication for which children are the specific audience but which adults can overhear . . . they suspend defences and listen – in a way secretly – as children. So long as the affection is there.'

The key word is 'affection'. When children read *What is the Truth?* the warm fellowship of all writers everywhere invades the classroom. In particular, they feel a kinship with the great poet and must follow in the family footsteps. Quite simply, he makes them want to write. This may not be one of the official attributes of the Poet Laureateship; I believe it was one of the most distinctive gifts Ted Hughes brought to the office. Now it is a richly enduring legacy to children.

As for the teacher, she may listen too, at first secretly, eavesdropper in the land of childhood, then openly, party to the creative complicity between poet and child. She too shares a measure of the grace.

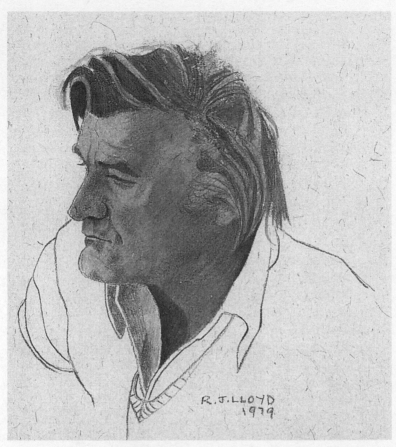

Portrait of Ted Hughes by R. J. Lloyd who illustrated
the first edition of *What is the Truth?*

In the Company of Shakespeare
and Ted Hughes

I had just finished directing Peter Schat's Opera *Houdini* for the Netherlands Opera in 1976. Free and relieved and feeling somewhat like an escape artist myself, I walked into the Atheneum bookshop in Amsterdam and saw, on the table in front of me, *A Choice of Shakespeare's Verse*, 'selected with an introduction by Ted Hughes'. I opened the paperback book and met his introduction. Incredible.

There it was: words for all those undefined things I did not understand but had felt so strongly and relied on during my productions of *A Midsummer Night's Dream*, *The Tempest* and an earlier choreographic collaboration with Alf Sjöberg on *Troilus and Cressida*.

Two days later, on the train from Gothenburg to Stockholm, literally on my way home, I started with the 'Selection'. I spoke to our theatre director and immediately began with the stage version *Soundings*: a soliloquy for one actress over seventy, with the great dramatic roles in the blood of her performing and personal self, with Ted's choice of Shakespeare's verse as the place of departure, his dramaturgical structure a base support calling on her own experiences for the binding element 'as she looks through them into her own darkness'. The production was performed in 1978 with Karin Kavli at the Royal Dramatic Theatre and two years later in Holland, titled *Ank van de Moer plays Shakespeare*.

I met Ted Hughes for the only time at his sister Olwyn's home in London. I had come to present the script. I remember most how he came down the stairs, his friendliness, his warmth and kind appreciation of the work that had been done. Encouraged, inspired and somewhat in awe I returned to Sweden. There followed performances of the 'Selection' in Sweden and Holland, and a long, on going telephone dialogue-conversation with Ted stretching over some nineteen years from my room in the theatre to Ted at Court Green, North Tawton.

In 1979 came the first letter: a twelve-page answer to my telephone call for help with *Measure for Measure*. It helped stabilize the performance while reassuring me that the play was at least as terrible and psychotic as I had thought.

In 1983 Ingmar Bergman returned from exile and opened with *King Lear*. It was made for an empty blood-red stage, with the promise that I would do the choreography. So Ted and I had a lot to talk about: conversations about *Lear*, Bergman, Euripides, Mishima, *Peer Gynt*, *The Winter's Tale*, our actors, Madame de Sade, the choreographic work, the choreographic spirit of Shakespeare's plays, etc. I liked it all very much.

In the winter of 1988, I spoke to Ted about extending the soliloquy idea to include a whole company of actors and something about the 'last fifteen plays'. By chance, this coincided with a new introduction Ted had to write to his selection of Shakespeare's verse. So now our conversations moved around these two poles. Then in the winter of 1989 Ted asked if I could briefly sum up in a letter what we had been talking about over the previous months, and after some weeks I sent him a one-and-a-half page sort of answer. About the same time I had a startling experience while improvising in a workshop with two ten-year-olds on 'Take, O take those lips away': beginning with just the physical effort of the saying of the words in English, then over to their rough Swedish translations, making it then possible for them to return to and 'use' the original text. Unforgettable – those months on the telephone with Ted, Shakespeare, and the voices of those two children.

The following year, after the introduction was done, Ted now asked if he could answer my letter by writing letters to me. Not understanding the implications at all, but feeling very flattered and quite proud, I said, 'yes'. Between 23 April and 14 June 1990 I received fifty-four letters from Ted – of varying lengths, mailed on five different occasions, prefaced with short notes. 'These letters became this book,' Ted wrote in the foreword to *Shakespeare and the Goddess of Complete Being*, which was published in 1992.

In September 1990, in the wake of Ted's letters and with his full support, I began a project with young people and Shakespeare's text in the classroom, based on Ted's selection in the American edition *The Essential Shakespeare*. (With Ted's help we received some 800 copies almost as a gift, to start us off.) Inspired by the tremendous input of Ted's letters, those two ten-year-old children, the enthusiasm of the actors, the teachers and class N3B, I had an uncanny feeling that if we had Ted's selection as our base, combined with the experience of the theatre version and script, this just all might lead up not just to a vast workshop for me and the actors but to a long-term education of a new audience for the theatre.

In 1991 the pupils in class N3B gave the first performance of a script based on material from *Soundings*, Ted's 'Selection' and his version of *A Midsummer Night's Dream*. It was the first of many such scripts used to train everyone: teachers, the actors, N3B, myself, our public. Prepared in the classroom, rehearsed at Dramaten (the Royal Dramatic Theatre) and performed at the House for Culture for thousands of students and their teachers as an introduction and invitation to the project. (This script later became 'Bottom's Dream' and 'Bottom's Second Dream' at Dramaten). It was also the beginning of what was to be called Will's Co., which by 1996 was the driving force of the work out in the schools.

In 1992–4 Ted sent me text excerpts from eleven of the 'fifteen' plays and a letter with suggestions about this play of Shake-speare's that we have never seen and never heard, guiding me and making clear the possibilities and importance of, as he called it, this 'invention' of mine: an education of groundlings and understanders, filled with Shakespeare learned by heart and forever in their mental and spiritual baggage. And we began in 1994 a wild experiment. The first collective performances in 'relay', with some two hundred students aged six to eighteen, from different schools, who had joined together to play, in English and by heart, Shakespeare's *The Tempest* in a version by Ted Hughes. What a gift! The experiment eventually culminated in 1998, when Stockholm was Culture Capital of Europe. Ted had ploughed the ground, so it was just to take the back stairs up to the kitchen, see how things had been done, and get to know him, Shakespeare/Ted. The sooner the better!

Preparations began in 1996 with a generous endowment from the Ministry of Education for the project 'In the Company of Shakespeare'. By the end of 1998 we had worked with over 5,000 students. The project involved classes, teachers, schools both inside and outside Sweden, thirteen 'relay' performances, fifty-four performances of 'Bottom's Dream' and 479 visits in schools. There was an inauguration on the main stage of the Royal Dramatic Theatre with actors, theatre directors, politicians, Will's Co. and classes of children performing, giving speeches, reading, reciting. And this is only a part of what was accomplished. We had been asked to do the impossible. And thanks to Ted, we did. Without him, none of this would have happened.

An eight-year-old asked if we could come back the following week and again be their guide to Shakespeare. I can feel like that child. But Ted doesn't have to come back next or any other week – he is already here, ever ready and waiting, in the 'Selection', in *The Goddess of Complete Being*, not to mention everything else he has written and done.

ROY DAVIDS

Ted Hughes's 'Sylvia Plath: The Evolution of "Sheep in Fog"' – The Onlie Begetter

'I'll try to send you something you may be able to use.' This throwaway remark by Ted Hughes concluded a discussion I had opened about poetical drafts during one of our summer afternoon drives through the Devon lanes. I had hoped at most for a few scraps that I might use in a lecture I was preparing for the forthcoming book collectors' weekend at Dove Cottage. Instead Ted hijacked the whole idea, made it entirely his own, and in less than a week produced this major, sparklingly written, critical essay, leaving me in (I must admit) the not unenviable role of attendant lord at the conception of a remarkable *tour de force*. Ted generously allowed me later to become the privileged custodian of all the manuscripts of the poem, which he has shown in this essay to be the key witness of the transition in mood and spirit from the *Ariel* poems to the extraordinary poetic outburst of the last thirteen days of Sylvia Plath's life, and also of the drafts of his own essay about it.

Ted's essay on 'Sheep in Fog' is one of the best analyses of the genesis and evolution of a poem. His own life as a poet, coupled with his intimate appreciation of Plath's work, as her mentor and monitor, and the survival of all the manuscripts, each dated, has enabled him to retrace the poem both in terms of its sources and its flowering in a way that, to my knowledge, is unequalled.

It is one of the best pieces Ted ever wrote on Plath's work and genius, partly because of the nature of the material and the manuscripts but also because it is so concentratedly about one poem and his treatment therefore moves from the particular to the general, a route often more telling than that from the general to the particular.

Ted's 'Sheep in Fog' essay is undoubtedly the best commentary on the nature and significance of poetical drafts. Here, as someone who has worked on and studied manuscripts for their own sake over a period of thirty-five years, I can perhaps speak with more authority than on the other aspects that I indicate in this note. No one else has written so eloquently or so perceptively on the importance of drafts, and why rather than being discarded they command respect as more than the 'incidental adjunct to the poem' – indeed 'they are a complementary revelation, and a log-book of its real meanings'. In the case of 'Sheep in Fog' the drafts 'have revealed the nature and scope of the psychological crisis that gives the poem its weird life, sonority, its power to affect us. In other words, they are, as the final poem is not, an open window into the poet's motivation and struggle at a moment of decisive psychological change.'

Ted's essay, is, moreover, one of the most penetrating exposures of the poetic impulse and the processes by which poems come or are dragged into being, common to the experience, he generously suggests, of all poets, at various times.

Lastly, the essay is a wonderful demonstration of Ted's own genius and vision, the subtlety of his responses, the depth of his understanding, the generosity of his sympathies and of the thrill and powerful richness of his prose.

The best thing that has ever happened to me is Ted and Carol's love – they have enhanced my life immeasurably, and have redefined for me the concept of friendship in terms of themselves.

Two Poets Laureate Joined by 2,000 Years

Ovid completed his *Metamorphoses* – which has since streamed through European culture – at about the time of the birth of Christ. I read the most recent translation while celebrating and thinking on that birth. What could be made of this coincidence of imperishable literature and lasting glory?

Ted Hughes's new working of the *Metamorphoses* is without doubt the most exciting, addictive collection of poems in English written in recent and not so recent times. They may well be the masterpiece of a poet whose profligacy and magnificent unfashionability have made him the object of sneers by some etiolated critics whose swotted degrees make them think of themselves as the arbiters of good writing.

They are mere midges. Hughes is a great poet. He can be bad, he can be poor, like all great poets. But at his best he can be called in with the very greatest – even with Wordsworth, our third poet, and sometimes with Milton, our second. Here, through Ovid, he challenges Shakespeare. Read Hughes's Ovid and know the depths of our inheritance. I am not a pundit, but let me push out the boat and guarantee that, like me, you will be awash with awe and newly alert understandings about the deep springs of our culture.

We are talking about the cave of Ali Baba, and so I will concentrate merely on the first few pages of Hughes's translation. I know that this is a technique beloved of lazy reviewers, so I assure you that the Pyramus and Thisbe who end Hughes's book are just as refashioned in his words as the opening pages.

But in the beginning is excitement – not in narrative as we see in the story of Phaeton or Echo and Narcissus, or the rape of Proserpina, or Tiresias (the most provocative analysis of sex ever printed) – but the excitement of the old joining hands with the new.

In short, Ovid's opening piece – The Four Ages – could be read as a preview of contemporary cosmology. Before I begin to quote, I am well aware that Hughes's version is his own re-creation; in his translation of Semele, for instance, he uses the phrases 'nuclear blast' and 'general deterrent'. 'Photon' also occurs, as well as other terms which must have been foreign to Ovid. Hughes wants to convince us now of Ovid – and by all the gods he does. The point is to make it work for us.

Space makes its miserly demands and so I have to be brief but in stanza two Hughes translates:

> Before sea or land, before even sky
> Which contains all,
> Nature wore only one mask –
> Since called Chaos –
> A huge agglomeration of upset

A few lines on he writes:

> Land, sea, air were all there,
> But not to be trodden or swam in
> Air was simply darkness,
> Everything fluid or vapour, form formless.

Come in Lee Smolin. Come in Sir Martin Rees, Astronomer Royal. Ovid 2,000 years ago was telling you about the beginning of the Universe.

> Heat fought cold, moist dry, soft hard, and the weightless
> resisted weight

Is this gravity? Newton is 1,600 years ahead.

And one last tag to show Ovid's Archimedean insight into a science which the Greeks might have invented.

Also resonating –
Each one a harmonic of the others. Just like the strings
That would resound one day in the dome of the tortoise.

Come in Pythagoras and the numbering of the Universe and
musical harmony.

I know that Ovid's gift to Chaucer and particularly Shakespeare is what makes him as immortal as any mere writer can
ever be. But this insightful cosmological beginning gives me as
much pleasure as the amazing stories of Semele and Tiresias.
Stories of gods becoming humans becoming animals becoming
gods becoming water becoming trees becoming monsters. All the
world seems to be in Hughes's Ovid, from the description of the
Beginning, which vies with Hawking and Genesis, to the
profound psychology of the violent passions of the gods and
their subjects.

I wanted to couple this great book – the best present I have
ever bought for myself – with the morning service in a plain
Anglican church in the valley below the cottage in which I have
lived for twenty-seven years. It is a tiny church with a graveyard
still only half full and in which I hope to be buried, surrounded
by the Cumbrian fells.

There were about fifty of us there at the 10 a.m. Christmas
morning service. Fifty just about packs the church. We severally, I
assume, believed in the child born in the year of the *Metamorphoses*. Just as amazingly as anything in Ovid, but also echoed in
him, we worshipped an immaculate birth, a resurrection and a
life to come.

For that hour, we defied our world of hot politics and blood-
exciting scandals and listened to words which, like those of Ovid,
have somehow percolated down 2,000 years. We listened also, as
it happened, to a two-month-old child brought to the church by
her young mother, muttering and occasionally crying aloud, a
text as powerful as the deepness of Ovid. Both bringing us tidings
of who we really are.

(This article first appeared in *The Times*.)

MARINA WARNER

Hoopoe

———

When my son Conrad was born I used to read aloud from *The Poet's Tongue* while he was feeding, holding the book in one hand and looking over his head at it. I had an idea that the leap and pulse of the lines, the shine and veils of colours in the very sounds of the language would nourish him in a different way, even though it was likely he couldn't understand a word; that his mind would be printed to a die that would somehow conduct the flow in his newborn head into lovely shapes and give him pleasure and comfort, excitement and satisfaction, as the poems did to me. Though I know the old magical superstition of 'maternal impression' is nonsense (thankfully) – I half believe it at the same time and used to try to think beautiful thoughts throughout my pregnancy. It was established family wisdom, for example, that because my mother had visited the Cairo Museum on a regular basis while she was expecting, my sister Laura was born with the domed skull, slender neck and long narrow limbs of an Egyptian goddess.

Auden and Garrett's inspired collection was followed – not superseded – by Seamus Heaney and Ted Hughes's *The Rattle Bag*, which came out when Conrad was five, as if just for him, and both anthologies continued to enliven bedtime rituals. We also read Ted Hughes's stories for children and his poetry. *Under the North Star* thrilled us:

Inside the Doe's tears, the frozen swamp.
Inside the frozen swamp, the Wolf's blood.
Inside the Wolf's blood, the snow wind.
Inside the snow wind, the Wolf's eye.
Inside the Wolf's eye, the North Star.
Inside the North Star, the wolf's fang.

('Amulet')

'That's fierce', said Conrad, with shining eyes, and wanted to hear it again.

Ted Hughes's poetry is often fierce; and what is fierce in literature for children is the quality that stamps *Beowulf* and Euripides and Seneca and Dante – and the Shakespeare of *Titus Andronicus;* it erupts as a pleasure of poetry from 'human passion *in extremis*', a phrase Hughes uses in the Introduction to *Tales From Ovid* (1997). Fierceness runs through grotesque and terrible acts born from the extremes of the fantastic: Grendel and his mother the mere-wife's bloodthirsty raids, mothers' cold-blooded murders of their own babies, cannibal banquets. Ted Hughes reinhabited this mythic, epic and heroic tradition in many ways in his varied work, not only in the writing for children. But his encounter with Ovid, in his versions of the *Metamorphoses*, seems to have beaten, purified and annealed his own fierceness to a new, intense radiance. It would not be putting it too strongly to say that Hughes found in Ovid a twin soul, someone with whom he could expose his own terrors and passions unguardedly, through whom he could speak without sounding a note of anachronistic atavism.

To do this, like any sibling, he had to overlook some qualities of his twin: his tone is less urbane than Ovid's, his comedy more ghastly, his lines are less measured (they are hacked and splintered, often to go with the stories), and the glaze on the language is more raku than slipware. But *Tales From Ovid* is thrilling poetry, with the magic capacity to strip the listener/ reader of all defences and catch us up in the tale as a child is carried on the rhythm of a line of verse to stare with wide eyes, whispering 'and what then?' as the story unfolds.

The present collection of *Metamorphoses* seemed to be caught in mid-flight when it appeared. I hoped there would be more and I'd assumed there would be, soon enough, though when I look back, I realize that the poet, if he had not known he was gravely ill, would probably have created a visible, shapely conclusion to the book before publishing it. It would have alighted towards the end, come full circle from the ectoplasmic origins evoked at the beginning. Ovid's final hymn to the Pythagorean credo of cyclical transformation and renewal would surely have summoned Hughes to his most Prospero-like enchantments. As it is, however, very near the end of *Tales From Ovid*, Hughes's magnificent rendering of 'Tereus' appears. This is usually thought of as the myth of Philomela, the nightingale, who was brutally violated, tortured and muted by Tereus, her brother-in-law, and 'has infested poetry ever since', as Francis Celoria comments caustically in his valuable edition of another mythographer, Antoninus Liberalis. Indeed, Ted Hughes refers to the traditional heroine twice in the Introduction, reminding us that in *Cymbeline*, Imogen is reading the tale in bed when Iachimo steals in to rape her; he also describes *Titus Andronicus* as the most Ovidian of Shakespeare's plays, and it is of course the one in which Lavinia is raped and maimed to the pattern of Philomela. But Hughes's version rightly singles out Tereus as the protagonist, the malefactor, the prime subject of transformation therapy, and his myth seems to have become, for Ted Hughes, the most Ovidian of Ovid's *Metamorphoses*.

Ovid doesn't offer any systematic classification for his transmutations. Telling 'how bodies are changed / Into different bodies' (as Hughes renders the first line) explains the cosmos, its origins, its relations, its purposes along Pythagorean lines, with souls surviving through time and migrating across genera: this principle, with its full freight of anti-Christian significance, can often be glimpsed in Hughes's poetry. But the changes of shape come in several kinds: benign, when the god or goddess expresses pity for a mortal and saves the victim through a transformation (Daphne turned into a laurel to save her from Apollo's pursuit);

malign, when the metamorphosis punishes a culprit for pre-sumption or folly; or, magical, as in 'Erysichthon', whose daughter possesses the gift of protean shape-shifting and can therefore escape at will in any form from the clients to whom her father panders her.

The story of Tereus and Philomela and Procne appears in Ovid towards the end of Book VI, in a group of tales containing some of the fiercest, most arbitrary and most horrifying of divine acts of vengeful rage, including Arachne's transformation into a spider by Minerva and Apollo's flaying of another unwise artist, the satyr Marsyas. But interestingly, it combines all the different effects of Ovidian metamorphosis, for when Procne is turned into a swallow 'with the blood still on her breast' and tongueless Philomela becomes a nightingale, the sisters escape from the story, from the likelihood of further bloodshed and violence: it is as if Oedipus and Jocasta had been spirited away by Sophocles and changed into doves rather than meeting their pitiless ends. And Philomela, whose tongue has been cut out, is rewarded when she discovers, outside the frame of the poem, the sweetest voice with which to mourn on behalf of human loss and folly (Keats is almost unique in hearing joy, not lamentation, in the nightingale's song). As for Tereus, the incestuous rapist, muti-lator and liar, as he pursues the sisters with sword drawn for vengeance, he finds himself unmanned, changed into a hoopoe, a bird whom Ovid clearly thinks of as distinguished for its look of violence with its long hooked beak and plumed helmet crest. So Tereus, too, is saved from the further consequences of his savage nature: his metamorphosis debases him, but gives him a place where he can no longer continue to do the harm he did as a man.

How does Ted Hughes write this fairytale reprieve? The sisters are fleeing Tereus:

> He came after them and they
> Who had been running seemed to be flying.

And suddenly they were flying. One swerved
On wings into the forest,
The other, with the blood still on her breast,
Flew up under the eaves of the palace.
Then Tereus, charging blind
In his delirium of grief and vengeance,
No longer caring what happened –
He too was suddenly flying.
On his head and shoulders a crest of feathers,
Instead of a sword a long curved beak –
Like a warrior transfigured
With battle-frenzy dashing into a battle.

Ovid's verbs pack less action: the sisters only hang from their wings, not swerve ('pendebant pennis'); the nightingale merely seeks the woods ('petit . . . silvas'); Tereus is 'velox' – swift – from grief, but governs no verb or active voice, being passively transformed ('vertitur in volucrem'). The vivid and impassioned simile of Hughes's last two lines with their hammering of the word 'battle' expand three very simple, even dull, words of Ovid's ('facies armata videtur') into a hectic, heightened image of a man berserk. (Hughes the naturalist also corrects, silently, Ovid's apparent belief that nightingales have red breasts!)

Ted Hughes's own process of metamorphosis points up throughout the Ovidian originals with fresh colour, taut rhythms, bright percussion (was he a Stravinsky, rescoring a Handel?). His English diction syncopates the sonorities of the Latin, catches the hexameter's long breath. But not all is louder and brighter and more pent up: the final stanza of his 'Tereus' reveals the enthralling quietness of his voice when he wanted to draw out the shape of the myth and modulate the screams and bellows of its mayhem to a mood of redemptive elegy:

He had become a hoopoe.
Philomela
Mourned in the forest, a nightingale,

Procne
Lamented round and round the palace,
A swallow.

These lines don't appear in Ovid, except as ghosts flitting between them.

Metamorphoses deny death and fold time; they bring ancient stories into everyday scenery and populate the landscape with living characters: to Pythagorean ears, Philomela doesn't only escape murder, she lives on in every nightingale. For Ted Hughes, time bent back against itself through poetry in the same way as Ovid's phenomena of nature are cast into new shapes by original miracles that suspended nature's laws. He commented that Ovid was interested in 'passion where it combusts, or levitates, or mutates into an experience of the supernatural', and that Tereus's tale is one in which 'mortal passion makes the breakthrough by sheer excess, without divine intervention'.

These birds haunted Hughes. On the bottles of Laureate's port for which he had commissioned a label, there appeared a watercolour of the crested hoopoe with its long curved beak: for Ted Hughes, Crow had been supplanted. When I noticed this and began thinking about what the myth of Tereus meant to him, I wrote a kind of fairytale short story called 'Lullaby for an Insomniac Princess', about trying to hear the song of the nightingale; on an impulse I sent it to Ted Hughes, in August 1998, because there seemed to be a connection. He wrote back:

Not sure I've ever heard a nightingale – or seen one. I've always lived beyond the bird's pale. Thousands of hours in woods at night – never heard a note. Once in S. Yorks rumour went through the school that there was a nightingale in some woodland near Conisborough. (Rather as you now hear the 'beast' has been sighted in some copse round here). Groups of enthusiasts were going out there. Eventually, I sat in there for a couple [of] hours and finally heard 3 piercing notes – but I could swear they were the squeals of dry brakes in the shunting yard down below the wood. That's as close as I've been.

I see there are only 4,000 nightingales left. But then. Friend of mine 20 years in Australia came back last week – visited me yesterday and almost his first words were 'where are all the birds?' then 'I was three days in London before I saw my first sparrow.' I've sat all afternoon in the orchard near the fountain that used to be crowded all day with birds. I didn't see a single bird till about 7 pm then a magpie flew across. Strange?

When the letter came I had no idea how ill he was, so I didn't understand till later why silence was on his mind.

KATHLEEN RAINE

Ted Hughes and Coleridge

A Choice of Coleridge's Verse, edited and introduced by Ted Hughes, is the modest title of the most remarkable essay, I believe, hitherto written on those few amazing poems that speak to the Imagination so irrefutably. Coleridge himself wrote that poetry speaks most powerfully when 'generally but not perfectly understood' and 'Kubla Khan' and 'The Rime of the Ancient Mariner' have been taken to heart in all their mystery by many generations who have made no attempt to decipher the symbolism of Coleridge's mythological landscape.

To my generation Livingston Lowes's *The Road To Xanadu* came as a revelation. Ted Hughes acknowledges with respect Lowes's contribution in this work of tracing Coleridge's powerful images to their sources in his reading and memories, presenting as he did in great detail the ingredients of those poems. But, as Hughes writes:

> Poems of this kind can obviously never be explained. They are total symbols of psychic life. But they can be interpreted – a total symbol is above all a vessel for interpretation: the reader fills it and drinks . . . Like the variety of potential readers, the variety of potential interpretations is infinite. Lowes's discoveries, then, explain nothing. But they do give interpretation a nudge.

Ted Hughes is prepared to go further, as only a poet of

Imagination is qualified to do. His remarkable insight into Coleridge's mind – a sequel to his *Shakespeare and the Goddess of Complete Being* – is a work of what one can only call 'the learning of the Imagination', something quite new in the criticism of works of literature, opening – or re-opening – as it does the neglected sources of poetic 'Inspiration' – to use a word not to be found in the vocabulary of modern critics, or indeed that of the majority of those today regarded as poets.

Ted Hughes's work brings us back to essentials. Coleridge calls the 'primary Imagination' the 'esemplastic power' that gives coherence and unity to all those potent images – to those great mythological poems. Whatever its ultimate source, inspiration is a reality; and Ted Hughes argues that 'Kubla Khan', 'The Rime of the Ancient Mariner' and 'Christabel', together with other poems constellated about them, are (amongst other things) 'a projected self-portrait of the poet's deepest psychological make-up. It is the myth of what made him a poet, but also of what destroyed him.'

In his earlier book on Shakespeare, Hughes revealed his power of profound penetration of the poetic imagination at work. The energy is erotic, specifically in the form of the Goddess. But whereas Shakespeare surrendered to her power, and was rewarded for his sacrifice by her gift of inspiration, Coleridge, in a similar confrontation, surrendered instead to Christian ortho-doxy, ever the enemy of Eros and of the Goddess, and the muse was revenged on him by the withdrawal of his poetic power. Coleridge, in the belief that religion was spiritual truth, severed the roots of his true spiritual life. Yet that fontal energy was great:

And from this chasm, with ceaseless turmoil seething,
As if this earth in fast thick pants were breathing,
A mighty fountain momently was forced:
Amid whose swift half-intermitted burst
Huge fragments vaulted like rebounding hail . . .

The Goddess, who first appears as 'woman wailing for her demon-lover', and the Abyssinian maid with her dulcimer, reappears in ever more menacing forms – 'the nightmare life-in-death' 'that thicks man's blood with cold', and at last as the sorrowful damned Geraldine against whose power the innocent Christabel's Christian virtues are unavailing. Thus Hughes puts together the pieces assembled by Lowes (with others put together by his own scholarly work) into a mythological story, a coherent dream. He makes use of Jungian psychology and of post-Jungian writers on the Goddess such as Joseph Campbell, Mircea Eliade, Ann Baring and Jules Cashford, and ideas of Shamanism now current, but whatever the ground on which he has built, Hughes's unfolding of the mythology of Coleridge's great poems is of an originality that places him in a class all his own, opening doors into a rich world of which we had been unaware, but recognize as soul's lost country.

With the perception only a poet can bring to the penetration of the sources of poetry, Hughes introduces his theme with a discussion of metrics – those haunting rhythms he himself thought new, but which were, on the contrary, old and native to the English language, emerging later in Hopkins's 'sprung rhythm'. Rhythms and metres which to the academic mind seem the work of artifice, are in reality the native speech of the soul, and evidence of her participation. In the absence of soul's inspiration the fountains do not flow. A.E. (author of *Song and its Fountains*) made this observation long ago, and went so far as to say that the use of metrics proper to this living source for trivial material and everyday matters is an inadmissible falsification. The absence of powerful metrics from so much modern verse is itself evidence of the absence of soul's participation, of inspiration from what one can only call higher levels of consciousness. Altogether Hughes's writings on imagination and its roots is radical, simple, powerful and profound. It is a recall to order, to the restoration of a dimension to the nature of poetry long absent from its discussion in our secular society.

It is sad that Hughes's death cut short what had seemed a maturing of his great gifts in a new dimension, but his contribution to the restoration of Imagination – in Coleridge's sense of the word – has been made and its transforming influence must continue. We owe him more than any other poet of his generation, for his transforming vision of the nature and purpose of imaginative writing.

With Sorrow Doubled

In Ted Hughes's masterly retelling of Ovid's retelling of the tale of Echo and Narcissus, Juno curses the nymph:

> 'Your tongue
> Has led me in such circles,
> Henceforth
> It will have to trail
> Helplessly after others, uttering
> Only the last words, helplessly,
> Of what you last heard.'

The curse of the circling (or doubling) tongue is transmitted to Echo like a fatal disease, so that when she falls in love with Narcissus and he, separated from his companions, calls to them: 'Where are you? / I'm here', she cannot speak for herself or do other than reply: 'I'm here,' and 'I'm here' and 'I'm here'.

A similar fate befalls Narcissus. A would-be lover, feeling 'mocked and rejected' (much as Juno had felt mocked and rejected), prayed:

> 'let him, like Echo, perish of anguish.'
> Nemesis, the corrector,
> Heard this prayer and granted it.

Meeting the face of a beautiful boy in a pool's 'limpid mirror', Narcissus imagines his love returned:

> Your face is full of love
> As your eyes look into my eyes
> I see it, and my hope shakes me.
> I stretch my arms to you, you stretch yours
> As eagerly to me. You laugh when I laugh.
> I have watched your tears through my tears.

We recognize the symptoms. He has contracted a form of Echo's disease: 'You laugh when I laugh', 'your tears through my tears'. Such linguistic doubling, reflecting the dramatic situation, has a cruelly ironic aspect. While seeming to promise a perfect union, it signals the reverse: insatiable longing, imminent death. In their disease's last stages, the sufferers come together as close as their cursed destinies permit.

> And when he moaned, 'Alas,' she wept,
> And groaned. 'Alas.' His last words,
> As he gazed into the dark pool,
> 'Farewell, you incomparable boy,
> I have loved you in vain'
> Returned from her lips with sorrow doubled:
> 'I have loved you in vain.'
> And after his last 'Farewell'
> Came her last 'Farewell'.

Hughes's echoic effects, obviously an essential feature of this particular story, are echoed in another of his Ovidian retellings, the tale of 'Arethusa'. As Narcissus had 'found [a] pool' and in its 'limpid mirror' fallen 'deeper and deeper in love', Arethusa

> found a stream, deep but not too deep,
> Quiet and clear – so clear,
> Every grain of sand seemed magnified.
> And so quiet, the broad clarity
> Hardly dimpled.
> The poplars and willows that drank at it
> Were doubled in a flawless mirror.

Plunging in, she is pursued by the river-god Alpheus, who, she tells Ceres,

> Poured himself into his true nature
> And mingled his current with my current.

Arethusa escapes, however, thanks to the intervention of the goddess Diana. Her last words – 'That is my story' – are echoed in a very different context, the last words of one of her remaker's *Birthday Letters*:

> You are ten years dead. It is only a story.
> Your story. My story.

The sorrowful doubling that is such a striking feature of the two 'Tales from Ovid' reappears as a structural principle – I am tempted to say *the* structural principle – of the later book (though some of the *Birthday Letters* predate the Ovidian Tales).

Their doubling begins with the two protagonists' first predestined meeting at the St Botolph's magazine party in Cambridge:

> Our magazine was merely an overture
> To the night and the party. I had predicted
> Disastrous expense: a planetary
> Certainty, according to Prospero's book.
> Jupiter and the full moon conjunct
> Opposed Venus. Disastrous expense
> According to that book. Especially for me.
> The conjunction combust my natal Sun.
> Venus pinned exact on my mid-heaven [. . .]
> That day the solar system married us
> Whether we knew it or not.

Their meeting is imaged in the 'St Botolph's' letter both by its linguistic doubling and by the double scar, a zodiac of tooth-marks with which she marks his face to match her own, much as Juno had marked Echo's voice. He remembers

The loose fall of hair – that floppy curtain
Over your face, over your scar. And your face
A rubbery ball of joy [. . .]

And the swelling ring-moat of tooth-marks
That was to brand my face for the next month.
The me beneath it for good.

The doubling intensifies in '18 Rugby Street', when they first meet as lovers:

You were slim and lithe and smooth as a fish.
You were a new world. My new world.
So this is America, I marvelled.
Beautiful, beautiful America!

This memory of the meeting of poets appropriately includes a memory of Donne remembering a similar ecstatic moment: 'O my America! my new-found land'.

When the scene moves to 'Your Paris' ('frame after frame / Street after street of Impressionist paintings') that city has two faces:

I kept my Paris from you. My Paris
Was only just not German. The capital
Of the Occupation and old nightmare.
I read each bullet scar in the Quai stonework
With an eerie familiar feeling [. . .]

We, too, read each scar 'With an eerie familiar feeling'. Returning to '9 Willow Street', the husband finds himself and his wife

Siamese-twinned, each of us festering
A unique soul-sepsis for the other,
Each of us was the stake
Impaling the other.

And in 'The Bird', a more sinister image of doubleness,

Your homeland's double totem. Germany's eagle
Bleeding up through your American eagle

takes the reader back to a Paris 'only just not German,' and forward to another war-zone, another structural pairing (in 'Black Coat'):

I had no idea I had stepped
Into the telescopic sights
Of the paparazzo sniper
Nested in your brown iris.
Perhaps you had no idea either,
So far off, half a mile maybe,
Looking towards me. Watching me
Pin the sea's edge down.
No idea
How that double image,
Your eye's inbuilt double exposure
Which was the projection
Of your two-way heart's diplopic error,
The body of the ghost and me the blurred see-through
Came into single focus,
Sharp-edged, stark as a target,
Set up like a decoy
Against that freezing sea
From which your dead father had just crawled.

I did not feel
How, as your lenses tightened,
He slid into me.

In 'A Picture of Otto', the enemies meet again, as doppelgängers, in the hellscape of Wilfred Owen's 'Strange Meeting':

Rising from your coffin, a big shock

To meet me face to face in the dark adit
Where I have come looking for your daughter.
You had assumed this tunnel your family vault.
I never dreamed, however occult our guilt,

Your ghost inseparable from my shadow
As long as your daughter's words can stir a candle.
She could hardly tell us apart in the end.
Your portrait, here, could be my son's portrait.

I understand – you never could have released her.
I was a whole myth too late to replace you.
This underworld, my friend, is her heart's home.
Inseparable, here we must remain,

Everything forgiven and in common –
Not that I see her behind you, where I face you,
But like Owen, after his dark poem,
Under the battle, in the catacomb,

Sleeping with his German as if alone.

A third structural pairing occurs in 'A Dream', 'The Minotaur', 'The Table', 'Dream Life', 'The Bee God', 'Blood and Innocence', 'Night Ride on Ariel', 'The Cast', and 'The God', as the daughter descends into her father's grave or he rises to join her. A fourth pairing, in 'Dreamers', involves her husband and another woman (also of part-German ancestry). The husband remembers seeing

The dreamer in her
Had fallen in love with me and she did not know it.
That moment the dreamer in me
Fell in love with her, and I knew it.

These last pairings, each with its mimetic repetitions, are reflections of the central one, the fatal conjunction of the I and the You; and are, of course, subsidiary to it. Each pairing operates on two planes, that of space and that of time: here and now, there and then, as at the end of 'The Blue Flannel Suit':

Now I see, I saw, sitting, the lonely
Girl who was going to die.
                              That blue suit,
A mad, execution uniform,

Survived your sentence. But then I sat, stilled,
Unable to fathom what stilled you
As I looked at you, as I am stilled
Permanently now, permanently
Bending so briefly at your open coffin.

There is a fifth and final pairing, one that gives Hughes's extended elegy for his wife the note of consolation that elegies traditionally offer. In the poem 'Fingers', his remember hers:

I remember your fingers. And your daughter's
Fingers remember your fingers
In everything they do.
Her fingers obey and honour your fingers,
the Lares and Penates of our house.

This is at once comforting and *dis*comforting. Even here, Hughes is too honest to deny Echo her voice as he remembers the linking of her fingers – and she, the linking of verbs, 'obey and honour' – in the marriage service.

As we come to terms with the desolate fact that his fingers are now as permanently stilled as hers, we can at least be grateful that, unlike so many poets who fall silent in their later years, Ted Hughes went out in the wake of two of his most moving and memorable books.

JOHN FOWLES

Ted Hughes: *Birthday Letters*

The summer of 1998 was remarkable for me since it married two outstanding poetry collections: Ted Hughes's *Birthday Letters*, and then in America Donald Hall's *Without*. They were both marvellous recreations by two sensitive men who had both suffered a similarly deep intensity of loss. Ted Hughes's star-crossed marriage with Sylvia Plath is of course endlessly well-known and often has been sadly misinterpreted. Donald Hall's marriage to Jane Kenyon was less well-known over here. I lost my own wife from cancer in 1990 and at least can vouch for the richness of both poets' sadness and how the two collections with their remarkable sensitivity can literally speak both for and to all of us who have been through the same unhappy experience of losing someone we loved. Together they seem to me to stand for something all we humans must undergo – basically the sadness and coldness, the ungivingness of the human condition. This is something we cannot avoid and again and again in their different ways these two men, such fine representatives of their countries' two poetries, have brought us in contact with the metaphysical reality of the human condition. Life can bring us nakedly close to what we are. This is very clearly a main purpose and function, almost a duty, of great poetry. I know the two poets very slightly and have long admired both of them. They have at this millennium made it difficult, if not impossible, not to recognize the agonizing darkness and remorselessness of our condition.

[145]

Now That We Live
by Jane Kenyon

Fat spider by the door.

Brow of hayfield, blue
eye of pond.
Sky at night like an open well.

Whip-Poor-Will calls
in the tall grass:
I belong to the Queen of Heaven!

The cheerful worm
in the cheerful ground.

Regular shape of meadow and wall
under the blue
       imperturbable mountain.

TOM PAULIN

'Your roundy face'

Part of the excitement of reading Ted Hughes's poetry and prose
is the sense that he is in urgent conversation with a whole series
of authors. Reading '18 Rugby Street' in *Birthday Letters*, I was
struck by these lines:

> And now at last I got a good look at you.
> Your roundy face, that your friends, being objective,
> Called 'rubbery' and you, crueller, 'boneless'.

The adjective 'roundy' stayed with me. I remembered a story I
once heard Seamus Heaney tell: how a schoolkid in County Cork
began an essay on the swallow by writing: 'The swallow is a
migratory bird. He have a roundy head.' The move between best-
behaviour, standard English and intimate spoken dialect –
between the official and the warmly oral – is touching. Hopkins
uses the word in 'As Kingfishers Catch Fire':

> As kingfishers catch fire, dragonflies draw flame;
> As tumbled over rim in roundy wells
> Stones ring; like each tucked string tells, each hung bell's
> Bow swung finds tongue to fling out broad its name.

Linking the two poems means that a void also opens up – stones
are falling down the roundy well with a sound like plucked
catgut knocking against the serried stones that rise up from the

darkness. Interestingly at the close of the sonnet, Hopkins uses the word 'faces':

> – for Christ plays in ten thousand places,
> Lovely in limbs, and lovely in eyes not his
> To the Father through the features of men's faces.

I like to think that in a certain type of heightened imagination, individual words or phrases in particular poems aren't simply being alluded to, but the whole poem. Hopkins's triumphantly religious sonnet, which has 'roundy' in its second line and 'faces' in its last, is compressed into the 'roundy face' which triumphs over the pejorative alternatives – 'rubbery' and 'boneless' – for her face. The phrase is redemptive and unique:

> Each mortal thing does one thing and the same:
> Deals out that being indoors each one dwells;
> Selves – goes itself; *myself* it speaks and spells,
> Crying *What I do is me: for that I came.*

This valuation of the individual is there in Hopkins's remark to Bridges: 'Every poet, I thought, must be original and originality a condition of poetic genius; so that each poet is like a species in nature (not an *individuum genericum* or *specificum*) and can never recur.' Thus there is a great tribute to Plath's genius concealed in that tender phrase, 'roundy face'. And the tenderness of the adjective is there in this couplet from John Clare's 'The Village Minstrel':

> Welcome red and roundy sun
> dropping lowly in the west.

The word belongs to dialect, to the spoken language that so inspired Hopkins, and which informs everything Ted Hughes wrote.

I catch another moment from Hopkins in these lines from 'Daffodils':

We workcd at selling them
As if employed on somebody else's
Flower-farm. You bent at it
In the rain of that April – your last April.
We bent there together, among the soft shrieks
Of their jostled stems, the wet shocks shaken
Of their girlish dance-frocks –
Fresh-opened dragonflies, wet and flimsy,
Opened too early.

Before the tense, stretched Degas-image, there is a reminiscence, I think, of this passage from Hopkins's journals:

The bluebells in your hand baffle you with their inscape, made to every sense: if you draw your fingers through them they are lodged and struggle with a shock of wet heads; the long stalks rub and click and flatten to a fan on one another like your fingers themselves would when you passed the palms hard across one another, making a brittle rub and jostle like the noise of a hurdle strained by leaning against; then there is the faint honey smell and in the mouth sweet gum when you bite them.

Both poem and prose involve flower stalks and jostling shocks – they remind me of Stanley Spencer, for this is an intensely English vision with a clear, cold, quietly redemptive light. Read in its entirety, behind the Hopkins's passage there is an almost subliminal religious iconography – hurdle, sheephooks, crook – and this informs the glistening sense of transience in the Hughes's lines to give a sense of tough, flexible permanence like a hurdle being leant against.

The third citing – or sighting – of Hopkins occurs in 'The Beach', where

The sea moved near, stunned after the rain.
Unperforming. Above it
The blue-black heap of the West collapsed slowly,
Comfortless as a cold iron stove

Standing among dead cinders
In some roofless ruin.

At the end of 'The Windhover', Hopkins shrugs his shoulders:

No wonder of it: sheer plod makes plough down sillion
Shine, and blue-bleak embers, ah my dear,
Fall, gall themselves, and gash gold-vermillion.

Here, apparently dead cinders break open and reveal a glowing
heart that is given a painterly inscape that is meant to remind us of
an Italian painting of Christ crucified. The pain is there in the
Hughes lines, but invisibly the uplift in Hopkins is there too. What
we find is a kind of allusiveness that has a fresh-peeled, sappy,
present-moment directness, as a line, a phrase, a whole poem, is
caught up in the current of Hughes's imagination, so that it both
lives again and imparts energy to the verse. What Hughes says of
Keith Douglas is also true of his own imagination:

There is nothing studied about this new language. Its air of
improvisation is a vital part of its purity. It has the trenchancy
of an inspired jotting, yet leaves no doubt about the
completeness and subtlety of his impressions or the thorough-
ness of his artistic conscience.

Hughes's introduction to his 1964 selection of Keith Douglas
brings out, I think, how the dead speak with tongues of fire in his
own poetry. His inspired tribute to Douglas makes us realize
that, like Hopkins, that young, hugely gifted poet lives on in
Hughes's writing, and that his poetry and prose is an invocation
and a celebration which exalts a whole community of writers and
readers – past, present and to come.

Portrait of me, made by Sylvia Plath, circa 1957

Ted Hughes

Portrait of Ted Hughes by Sylvia Plath from the collection of Roy Davids. Not to be further reproduced without permission of Roy Davids.

CLAIRE TOMALIN

'Daffodils'

Milton's 'Lycidas', Tennyson's 'In Memoriam', Hardy's poems of 1912–13 commemorating the girlhood of his first wife and his youthful love for her, are three of the great elegiac pieces in our language. Now another has joined them, Ted Hughes's *Birthday Letters,* a sequence of poems written for his wife Sylvia Plath, who killed herself during a period of angry estrangement between them, in the bitter month of February 1963. The bleak fact is known to everyone who cares for poetry, for she was a supremely gifted poet, with a voice entirely her own: strong, upsetting and beautiful. All the more difficult to achieve what Hughes has done, which is to do justice both to her and himself. Her voice is there, her nerviness, her rage, their fierce, awkward love, their youth, their children, what he calls the time when 'Our lives were still a raid on our own good luck'.

Hughes wrote the poems over a period of many years, and finished and published them at the end of his life. Each has a core of imagery that bites into the imagination. 'Daffodils', with its most correct of English titles, is about how they cut and sold the drifts of flowers growing round their Devon house in the last spring of Plath's life. The daffodils are not merely frail dancers, Hughes characteristically shows us their 'raw butts in bucket water, / Their oval, meaty butts', and tells us how they were sold for sevenpence a bunch to

> Old Stoneman the grocer,
> Boss-eyed, his blood-pressure purpling to beetroot
> (It was his last chance,
> He would die in the same great freeze as you).

Nothing tranquil about these memories. Hughes writes

> Nobody else remembers, but I remember.
> Your daughter came with her armfuls, eager and happy,
> Helping the harvest. She has forgotten,
> She cannot even remember you.

But he lives with memory, and gives it to us. He finds the significance of every detail. He remembers how they lost their 'wedding-present scissors' as they worked. Every year since that spring, he reflects, the daffodils have lifted again

> to forget you stooping there
> Behind the rainy curtains of a dark April,
> Snipping their stems.

> But somewhere your scissors remember. Wherever they are.
> Here somewhere, blades wide open,
> April by April
> Sinking deeper
> Through the sod – an anchor, a cross of rust.

Grief is the most difficult thing to write about, but the rusting scissors in the earth under the perennial flowers are true emblems of grief and time. Hughes is as formidable as he is brave.

PETER BROOK

———

One day, when we were working together on *Orghast,* Ted Hughes explained to me how he found the words in the new language that he was inventing for us. 'I listen,' he said, 'to the patterns that arise in the deep level of the brain, when impulses become sounds and syllables – and before they shape themselves into recognizable words.'

This capacity to be in touch with the vast complex of movements that underline all of human existence is what made Ted, Ted. Whether it was in bird life, the animal world, mythology, personal relations, literature or Shakespeare, Ted, like a neurosurgeon, saw straight through to the essential fibres. For this reason, logical language can never capsulate him. To find Ted, we must pause and listen to the powerful music behind the simple name Ted Hughes . . ..

SIR JOHN GIELGUD

In 1968 I was engaged by the National Theatre to play the part of Oedipus under Peter Brook's direction in a newly translated version of Seneca's tragedy. The whole company, headed by Irene Worth and myself, were gathered together in the very unattractive huts in a back street near Waterloo Station which the National was using as rehearsal rooms and offices while our performances were given at the Old Vic during the building of the big new theatre. We were about eighteen strong and sat crammed into one of the small dressing rooms while Ted Hughes, who had translated the play, proceeded to read it aloud to us. Kenneth Tynan, in a white high-necked sweater, roamed up and down the creaky passage, and looked in on us from time to time. Hughes's reading, which only lasted about 40 minutes, was an electrifying experience, and we huddled together spellbound by the power of the play itself and especially by the poet's brilliant handling of the material. Though I am ashamed to admit it, I very seldom read poetry though of course as an actor I have come to know something of its magic possibilities. I had read some of Ted Hughes's verses in various articles and interviews and had been greatly struck by his vividly imaginative approach towards nature and his own particular drive and power. I am so proud to have been involved in this Oedipus production and to have heard it liberated by Hughes's own unique personality.

IRENE WORTH

———

Ted Hughes was a mythic man, powerful and kind. From his great talent he drives forth poetry of a unique candour and hurricane force. With Hughes's 'elastic of life' his recent works from Aeschylus, Seneca, Ovid, Shakespeare, shake us up with joys and not the least of them is in the theatre. As for Theatre itself, I think of the story ('The Rain Horse') of the stalking, malignant horse in the field with an evil eye and pure hate of the trespassing stranger. It is as frightening as a gangster film.

I haven't the dates to hand when I recorded some of the plays of Shakespeare at Cambridge with Dadie Rylands and Tony White. I might perhaps have met Hughes then. I met so many interesting people there. I once asked Thom Gunn 'Are you all still twenty-eight?' and he said 'No – we're all a little older now.' However in 1957 we had the impact of *The Hawk in the Rain*, then *Lupercal*. Ten years later I had the happy experience of meeting and working with Hughes in Peter Brook's masterpiece production of Seneca's *Oedipus*. Brook had planned the play for John Gielgud as part of the new National Theatre still housed at the Old Vic. Ted adapted it. The production came about tentatively and is fully described in the prefaces to the published version by Hughes and Anthony Turner. They and Peter Brook emerged from a delicate problem with superb tact and grace.

Seneca's simplicity was formidable. So was Ted's. He seemed to write around us as characters and was probably inspired by our eccentric improvisations at rehearsal. He beat out short, hard phrases, stoic and strong. After Ted wrote Jocasta's death speech he read it to us. I don't ever want to lose that sound, Ted reading aloud. He read with a skill that cracked open words as though he had just invented them, right in the centre, as Margot Fonteyn did with Time. I believe that is when Ted taught me to act. He taught me to feel the freedom in words, not their enmity. Ted had made a mighty speech for Jocasta about birth which I simply wasn't up to. He guided me in the kindest, subtlest way, but I'm afraid I let him down. I should have been monumental and mammoth. Alas, I was only Whistler's Mother, but he set me on a search I have never abandoned. I hear John Gielgud's voice at the close of the play: harsh, volcanic, majestic and brave, 'Lead me'. Early in rehearsal Gielgud had contributed considerable merriment regarding Jocasta's suicide. I had suggested my death would be easier if the obelisk/sword was on a plinth. And the lovely voice of John in the wings called out 'Plinth Philip or Plinth Charles?'

Shortly after *Oedipus* Hughes joined us in Paris, where Peter Brook was assembling international actors for his experimental company. In those days we worked at the Gobelin factory and Ted, through his profound scholarship, invented a way for us to develop a new language. Peter was exploring the use of emotive sound in communication. Ted helped us with his incredible quickness and improvisation toward words, scrambled out of an Indo-European root. He gave us an armature on which to hang new words. The procedure inevitably became glib, but if Hughes was disappointed he gave no sign, and I do not think the experiment was wasted. Perhaps one can find traces of the idea in his Introduction to *A Choice of Shakespeare's Verse*.

An actor has words to learn and reveals them through emotion. The poet deals with emotion through words alone. Ted's words and the way they lie on the paper nourish us as nature nourished him. He does not write about nature but within nature. He picks up a badger's tooth, bleached and beautiful, is bitten by a mosquito, understands the law in the country of cats.

He is a magician. A dove flies out. He gives us liberty. We become the jaguar with 'horizons under his feet'.

His curiosity keeps him on the wing. He deals with adversity and sorrow. He understands and has written about the profound 'nothing' of Cordelia. He knows that the heart's truth is inexpressible for most of us.

I read Ted's words, his prose and poetry, with thanksgiving and I am moved by his 'proud full sail', but like his otter I melt into the water.

A rare tree has fallen. The forest has taken the forester. Thank you for your bounty, dear Ted. We hold you dear.

LAVINIA GREENLAW

The Death of Hippolytus

━━━━━

Although Ted Hughes's *Phèdre* is a version of a version (from Racine, from Euripides), there is nothing diluted or distant about it. He expands the play's reach and electrifies its tensions. As tragedy, *Phèdre* has a fatedness that is more innate than the will of the gods and more collective than hamartia, any individual fatal flaw. Racine's vision is well matched in that of Hughes, who can see beyond the human scale while touching the core of human nature.

Everybody is torn apart; Hippolytus most of all and, in the end, literally so. He loves his father, his father's enemy and his state; and he is struggling with the implications of his step-mother Phèdre's passion for him. 'O you mighty gods in heaven,' he implores after she has declared herself, 'If there is a hole in your creation, / Drop this secret through it.' Hughes is attuned to the Shakespearean nature of Hippolytus's fate – the damnation that comes with knowledge upon which one is unable to act.

The tragedy takes place at the deepest level of consciousness without allowing its subjects the ease of oblivion. They see what they're doing, they know what's coming but they don't understand it and cannot help themselves. This is visceral emotion, something Hughes amplifies by uncoupling Racine's rhymes, dispensing with the symmetry of his alexandrines and using a mercurial irregular meter instead. As ever, he pares down the language and finds words that, in their weight and clarity, drop like stone.

As the characters are paralysed by their various dilemmas, Hughes galvanizes the atmosphere with onomatopaeic verbs: 'buzz', 'dash', 'swift', 'snatch', 'waft', 'grope', 'groan'. He intensifies activity – having Hippolytus 'hurtling along the sands' and 'scouring the woods' – and demands more from the senses. Where Crete was remembered as red with the blood of the Minotaur, he has it 'reeking'. Where Phèdre goes hot and cold, he has her complaining: 'My whole body scorched, then icy sweat'. There is a layer of modern language, too, that helps to connect the audience with the psychology of the play: 'anaesthesia', 'self-control', 'incoherent', 'mania', 'rapist'.

I saw *Phèdre* during its first run at the Albery Theatre in September 1998. The set was a bleak ante-room or corridor: a place where paths crossed and lives were suspended. A towering window, filled with the light and shadow and sound of the sea, belittled every scene. The set and clothes were sombre, earthy or metallic, and austere. Apart from Phèdre, who toppled and span, the actors were mostly still. It was a visually restful production that enabled you to listen to the words and trace their effect. Most powerful, was the moment that Theramène (David Bradley) narrated the death of Hippolytus.

Nobody can drag out of Hippolytus exactly what they want. He is torn to pieces after his father, Theseus, invokes Neptune to punish him for supposedly sleeping with Phèdre. Theramène has returned to tell Theseus that his wish has been granted, an agonizing monologue that Hughes has slowed to the point where Theseus (and the audience) is forced to contemplate each unbearable step. The story stops and starts as hope wavers and returns, and the rhythms correspondingly ebb and surge. In the initial moment of the doomed journey, tiny noises,a 'jingle' and 'click', amplify the silence.

There is something universal in Hughes's plainspeaking and reflexiveness: 'His mood made the mood of every man.' In the same way, the monster that rises out of the sea becomes every monster, archetypal and elemental. It hits us first as a wave of sound, a 'bellow' and 'groan', and then materializes as 'a mountain of water' which collapses back into sound, 'a solid fall of thunder'. This is a something you hear with your whole body; it rattles every molecule like a bomb going off. Before we have even seen the monster, it is beyond perceiving. Then it takes shape: first as a simple 'beast' and then as a poly-mythical combination of dragon and bull. Its mouth is a cavern of roaring water, bonding it with its source.

What is to come is palpable. 'We breathed a mist of horror', and there is no room for heroics: 'Weapons or courage were out of the question'. A moment of possible escape blossoms, 'like a miracle', but it isn't one. Badly injured by Hippolytus's lance, the monster sweeps away the wheels of his carriage with a flick of its tail, an immortal afterthought. At this point, Theramène qualifies things: 'What came next I can hardly credit. I did not see it.' The word 'credit' is slipped in in a familiar phrase but resounds with a question of belief. Like Theramène, we are being asked to believe in what we have not seen, something that even for those who saw it was unbelievable.

The horrific end of Hippolytus, dragged across the rocks by his frenzied horses, is portrayed with an absolute simplicity that emphasizes his diminishing substance in comparison to the gods. He was 'Bounding like a bucket behind them' . . . 'Then it was two wild horses dragging a man' and, finally, '. . . a weightless bundle . . . He signed every stone'. When the grieving Theseus concludes that 'Inexorable. That is the word for the gods', Hughes once again chooses a strikingly modern word that adds dimensions with its etymology, in this case, of being impervious to entreaty.

By the end of Theramène's speech, I was weeping and exhausted. The words affected me on a level unmediated by analysis or thought. In doing so, the play revived my imagination which had, for some time, been a locked room. Perhaps I had been protecting myself from the slew of imagery and information we face every day and the etiolating layers (screens, wires, reportage) through which it reaches us. For a long time, nothing had felt as immediate as this story within a story. I am not the only person who has been opened or re-opened by Ted Hughes's work in this way. He was a pole star. We continue to set our compass by him.

TIM SUPPLE

First sighting: a tall and reserved figure – too large for our tiny, rabbit-warren corridors – being ushered through the Young Vic before a performance of *The Iron Man*. *The Iron Man* was not great theatre. It is difficult to stage, so the adaptation was flawed, the staging uncertain.

First impression: the old *Observer* colour supplement. A source of early knowledge in serials about the Kennedys, the Andes plane crash and Ted Hughes's *Orghast*. In those days the name Peter Brook meant nothing, neither did that of Ted Hughes actually. But the concept of a language-made-up and its experiment in a faraway desert alerted me. Why? Perhaps because I could not pin it down: partly poetry, not really interesting to me yet; partly a new language, quite interesting to me in the same way as a visit to a Viking exhibition might interest me; partly the connection with an ancient civilization, very interesting, fascinated as I was with Egypt, Atlantis and all things buried; and partly theatre, very interesting in proscenium-arch Victorian buildings housing Peter Pan or dull but impressive Shakespeare. What was this? Theatre as a new language, in a desert on a journey.

First impact: researching the *Oedipus* plays for a version at the Young Vic, I read Ted's Oedipus. Immediately I recognized one of the finest theatrical texts I had come across. I devoured it: its furious pulse, unique typography and (a hallmark I now recognize) this almost unbearable clarity: the moment of thought seen in the moment of speech glaring with an unavoidable definition. My heart soared and then fell. Nothing I would produce would have the bare-knuckle force.

First came the impression, then the impact, and then the sighting.

4/11/98

When I started writing this piece Ted Hughes was alive. Now he is dead and I must start again. Yesterday he was laid to rest. His huge, observant, kindly bulk lay for an hour or so in a box too small, surely, to hold him. In a church in Devon great, great sadness observed his strange silence, his strange immobility.

To me, Ted always seemed most interested in the primitive flash: the sudden flare of rage or passion that takes us and makes us act or speak despite our rational will and that drives us to our death. This is what he spoke most of on the stage: actors possessed, characters carried away, moments alive with meaning greater, older, deeper than a first glance could reveal. The bride and Leonardo hurling towards destruction, driven by an irrepressible lust in *Blood Wedding;* Moritz scratching and picking at his own curiosity until he stumbles across his own suicide in *Spring Awakening*. And everyone in Ovid's *Metamorphoses* – Myrrha, Tereus, Philomela, Semele, Pentheus, Midas – transformed by the heat of their own desire.

People changed into birds, flowers, the earth itself because their lust for another or for revenge cannot be contained in human shape, experience and language. What could be more essentially Ted Hughes than these Ovid stories?

His great skill, however, lay in his details, his sense of the specific. His words are nails, their meaning deep and fast. He saw this in Shakespeare – this ability to say it once, and again so we might see it better, and once more to really pin it down. And he had this himself: a vocabulary, a sharp curious mind that would move from word to word until it was clear and concrete.

To make it clear, to render it unshakeable and specific – what a great purpose for the theatre. But then to see what it is: to recognize that the sum total of words and actions reach mythic, primitive force, that theatre can be a sensation that leaves us breathless and shattered. This was the challenge with Hughes and his work. As he said of Shakespeare and of Ovid – theatre on two simultaneous planes; each moment psychologically credible, real and concrete, and yet each moment mythic.

More than anything this seemed to me to be his project in the short time I knew him. As he would say of other writers, this was his story – his fierce centre from which all things come.

This appears to be the great light which illuminates *Birthday Letters*: personal, specific and clear moments from life riddled with doom, gods, ghosts, the supernatural: Myth. Folk stories. Private life, inner worlds, poetry, drama as folk stories. Childlike. Magnificent.

While we were working on Wedekind's *Spring Awakening* Ted told me that he considered Lorca's essay 'Theory and Function of the Duende' to be the unsurpassed articulation of the possibilities of Theatre: 'All that has dark sounds has *Duende*. A mysterious power which everyone feels and which no philosopher can explain. There is no map, no formula to seek the *Duende*.'

And he told, unforgettably, the story that sits at the heart of Lorca's essay. Of La Nina de Los Peines, a singer in a bar in Cadiz who sang with all her skill but left the listener unmoved. But then an old man in the corner muttered 'Viva Paris' as if to say: Here we don't care about talent, or technique, or mastery. We care for something else.

Then La Nina de Los Peines jumped up like a madwoman, crippled like a medieval mourner, drank in one gulp a large glass of fiery cazalla, and sat down to sing without a voice, without breath, without subtlety, with a burning throat, but . . . with *duende*. To do it she needed to destroy all the scaffolding of the song and make way for a furious and blazing duende, fiend of the desert winds, that made the listeners tear their clothes with almost the same rhythm as West Indians and their rites, crowded before St Barbara's statue.

La Nina de los Peines had to wrench her voice, because she knew that the fastidious listeners wanted not forms but the essence of form. Pure music with hardly a body to hold itself up in the air. She had to weaken her own skills and safeguards, to get away from her muse and remain defenceless, so that her duende would come and deign to fight her hand-to-hand. And how she sang! She didn't play with her voice now, her voice was a jet of blood dignified by grief and sincerity, and it opened like a hand with ten fingers through the pierced but stormy feet of a Christ by Juan de Juni.

The coming of the *duende* always presupposes a deep change in the old forms. It gives a sense of freshness, totally unknown before, with a quality of the newly created rose, of miracle. It succeeds in producing an almost religious fervour.

Ted Hughes's belief and hope in theatre lay there.

MICHAEL HOFMANN
'Remembering Teheran'

———

How it hung
In the electrical loom
Of the Himalayas – I remember
The spectre of a rose.

All day the flag on the military camp flowed South.

In the Shah's Evin Motel
The Manageress – a thunderhead Atossa –
Wept on her bed
Or struck awe. Tragic Persian
Quaked her bosom – precarious balloons of water –
But still nothing worked.

Everything hung on a prayer, in the hanging dust.

With a splash of keys
She ripped through the lock, filled my room, sulphurous,
With plumbers –
Twelve-year-olds, kneeling to fathom
A pipeless tap sunk in a blank block wall.

*

I had a funny moment
Beside the dried-up river of boulders. A huddle of families
Were piling mulberries into wide bowls, under limp, dusty
  trees.

All the big males, in their white shirts,
Drifted out towards me, hands hanging –
I could see the bad connections sparking inside their heads

As I picked my way among thistles
Between dead-drop wells – open man-holes
Parched as snake-dens –

Later, three stoned-looking Mercedes,
Splitting with arms and faces, surfed past me
Warily over a bumpy sea of talc,
The uncials on their number-plates like fragments of
    scorpions.

*

I imagined all Persia
As a sacred scroll, humbled to powder
By the God-conducting script on it –
The lightning serifs of Zoroaster –
The primal cursive.

*

Goats, in charred rags,
Eyes and skulls
Adapted to sunstroke, woke me
Sunbathing among the moon-clinker.
When one of them slowly straightened into a goat-herd
I knew I was in the wrong century
And wrongly dressed.

All around me stood
The tense, abnormal thistles, desert fanatics;
Politicos, in their zinc-blue combat issue;

Three-dimensional crystal theorems
For an optimum impaling of the given air;
Arsenals of pragmatic ideas –

I retreated to the motel terrace, to loll there
And watch the officers half a mile away, exercising
  their obsolete horses.

A bleaching sun, cobalt-cored,
Played with the magnetic field of the mountains.

And prehistoric giant ants, outriders, long-shadowed,
Cast in radiation-proof metals,
Galloped through the land, lightly and unhindered,
Stormed my coffee-saucer, drinking the stain –

At sunset
The army flag rested for a few minutes
Then began to flow North

*

I found a living thread of water
Dangling from a pipe. A snake-tongue flicker.
An incognito whisper.
It must have leaked and smuggled itself, somehow,
From the high Mother of Snows, halfway up the sky.
It wriggled these last inches to ease
A garden of pot-pourri, in a tindery shade of
  peach-boughs,
And played there, a fuse crackling softly –

As the whole city
Sank in the muffled drumming
Of a subterranean furnace.

And over it
The desert's bloom of dust, the petroleum smog, the
  transistor commotion
Thickened a pink-purple thunderlight.
The pollen of the thousands of years of voices
Murmurous, radio-active, rubbing to flash-point –

*

Scintillating through the migraine
The world-authority on Islamic Art
Sipped at a spoonful of yoghurt
And smiling at our smiles described his dancing
Among self-beheaded dancers who went on dancing
     with their heads
(But only God, he said, can create a language).

Journalists proffered, on platters of silence,
Split noses, and sliced-off ears and lips –

*

Chastened, I listened. Then for the belly-dancer
(Who would not dance on my table, would not kiss me
Through her veil, spoke to me only
Through the mouth
Of her demon-mask
Warrior drummer)

I composed a bouquet – a tropic, effulgent
Puff of publicity, in the style of Attar,

And saw myself translated by the drummer
Into her liquid
Lashing shadow, those arabesques of God,

That thorny fount.

. . . would I know there were such a place, with three old walnut trees, near Isfahan? Is there?

James Buchan

Who will dare to say to me that this is
  an evil foreign land.

Anna Akhmatova

What follows, a little apologetically, is a microcosm of what seems to me the most important development in English letters over the last decade or so, namely the re-emergence or rediscovery of Ted Hughes. *Mutatis mutandis* – with different readers and different poems (although, obviously, I love 'my' poem!) – it should be imagined as enacting itself thousands of times up and down the country, and abroad. The personal part of it, that which concerns me, is unimportant and accidental, and is offered with some embarrassment.

I was born in 1957, the year *The Hawk in the Rain* was published. At school in the 1970s, I was given poems of Hughes to read (never the best way – it's still put me off Auden and Larkin). I supposed for a long time that he, an Englishman of a peculiar deep Englishness and a writer on animals and elemental subjects, just didn't have much to say to me, a German of a peculiar shallow Englishness and a writer on human and anecdotal subjects. I bought his books, but didn't read them much.

One day in the *Times Literary Supplement* – it was on page 3 – I saw a poem that changed all that for good. I don't know what poem it was, maybe 'Walt' or 'For the Duration' or 'The Last of the 1st/5th Lancashire Fusiliers', something about a relative who had survived World War I. Thenceforth, I read Hughes differently – as a contemporary, one of the three or four poets whose books I waited for, and who made every one else faintly superfluous. His prose – the huge book on Shakespeare, the sublimely intelligent and unconventional writing in *Winter Pollen* – the poems at the end of the 1995 *New Selected Poems*, the Ovid versions he did, first for James Lasdun and me, and then in his own *Tales From Ovid*, and the irresistible *Birthday Letters*. This tremendous surge of creative work finally and belatedly – in the eyes of my co-generationists and me – brought Hughes out from under the everlasting 1960s and his extended tenure of the Laureateship.

I haven't, in the end, chosen 'Walt', or anything from Ovid, or one of the *Birthday Letters*, or that amazing poem-cum-deficit-reckoning called 'The Other', but one of the earlier, uncollected, pieces from the *New Selected Poems,* called 'Remembering Teheran'. It mattered to me to get a sense of approaching something if not new, then at least disregarded, or beyond the pale.

In many ways, it contradicts one's received idea of Hughes. It's not about England or about animals, it's funny and occasional (as I remember him writing somewhere that almost the whole recent output of the Western tradition has become), and exotic and diagnostic, and it deploys the poet himself in it as a kind of pawn. It is very much 'my kind of poem'. I wish I'd written it. More to the point, it's the kind of thing Lawrence might have written on his travels, in Germany or Italy or Australia or Ceylon or New Mexico – and perhaps did write, although I couldn't find any especially close analogy, not in Lawrence's poems anyway. Perhaps it's not too surprising that Hughes didn't include it in any of his books of the period (if I understand the arrangement of the *New Selected Poems*, he wrote it in the 1970s): it would tend to 'fall outside the frame', as you say in German. On the other hand, it would be a natural for any anthology of 'abroad thoughts', of expatriation, of centrifugal musings and scrutinies. Think how well it would go with Elizabeth Bishop's poems about Brazil, Bunting's 'Aus Dem Zweiten Reich', Cummings's poem about the police and the Communists in Paris, Brodsky's divertimenti from Italy, Mexico or England, or – I think, best of all – with Robert Lowell's 'Buenos Aires'. It's a type of poem that comes to us from the Romantics, from Shelley's 'Mont Blanc' and Goethe's 'Roman Elegies', but touristically and culturally and interrogatively extended by our century; where the unsettled self takes its bearings ('In my room at the Hotel Continental / a thousand miles from nowhere' – Lowell) and shyly or intrepidly goes out to encounter a changed world that reflects it differently, better, or perhaps not at all. 'Je' is not 'un autre' – perhaps, think of Bishop or Brodsky, is even more 'je' than it ever could be 'at home' – it is 'ailleurs', and perhaps nowhere more so than in 'Remembering Teheran'.

The poem is spun out of Hughes's nerve-endings. 'How it hung', it starts, itself hanging, echoing Sylvia Plath's desert poem 'The Hanging Man' and, more dimly, Dylan Thomas's 'I sang in my chains like the sea'. Prometheus is not far to seek.

> How it hung
> In the electrical loom
> Of the Himalayas – I remember
> The spectre of a rose.

(How incredibly beautifully, by the way, Hughes writes free verse: the breaths of the first two 'h's, heavily, almost reluctantly muted into the drone of 'hung', 'loom' a foreshadowing of 'Himalayas', 'electrical' generating 'spectre', the Persian picture-postcard prettiness of 'rose' countermanded and finally more menacing than anything else. Isn't this tensile music Poe or Tennyson by other means?) In another poem, that 'hanging' might have been used for the structuring of the whole piece, and Hughes uses the word three more times, and maybe its presence is felt further in the army flag resting 'for a few minutes', and in the water 'dangling from a pipe', but the growth of the poem outstrips even such a helpless and *dégagé* thing as hanging. Nor is it bracketed by the flag that, at sunset, 'rested for a few minutes then began to flow North' (how proud any dissident East European or South American poet would be of the two contrasting coats of the pathetic and the automatic in those glorious lines!). Instead, the poem keeps being broken open, again and again, by the pressure of its strange and abundant material. In an odd way, it gets out of sync with itself. It has its funny moment in the delicious story of the blind tap in Hughes's room and the squad of baby plumbers sent in to 'fathom' it – and then an asterisk, and then 'I had a funny moment'! Unforgettable things crowd into the poem: the three 'stoned-looking Mercedes' (a pure droll outrageous equivocation between the two senses of 'stoned' – but no more than 'loom' at the beginning is equivocal too: it's as though what Hughes sees and experiences is so strange, he needs to call upon words in many different senses all at once) that bring back a decade of newsreel from Beirut; the gorgeous Latinity of 'Eyes and skulls / Adapted to sunstroke'; the naked vulnerability of 'I knew I was in the wrong century / and wrongly dressed' (a little like Lowell's 'I was the worse for wear'); the Lowellian pairing of 'the tense, abnormal thistles' – as indeed much of the poem is reminiscent of Lowell, and a line like 'In the Shah's Evin Motel' *is* Lowell just as much as 'In Boston the Hancock Life Insurance Building's / beacon flared' is Lowell; the clever, helpless agglomerations of language, thickening and emulsifying, in 'The desert's bloom of dust, the petroleum smog, the transistor commotion' (what a humming line!); to the beautiful line – which wouldn't look out of place in Crane (or hemicrane) or Eliot – 'scintillating through the migraine' to the final discord, 'That thorny fount'.

Necessarily, I think, the poem of a foreign place, or the poem of the self in a foreign place (the house that Jack didn't build), is a poem of incomplete witness. Lowell's 'Buenos Aires' is an intermittent line drawn around next to nothing: leather, abrasiveness, neo-classical curves, 'frowning, starch-collared crowds' (strangely both like and unlike the 'cowed, compliant fish' in 'For The Union Dead'). 'Remembering Teheran' has an electrifying diligence about it, a continual openness to impressions, to terror, to strangeness, to awe. As it takes you through politics, religion, sex, history, technology, climate, geography and what all else, it takes up imagery drawn from thunder, drought, electricity, music, malfunction, plants and insects, and harmonizes them, so that the reader loses his sense of these things originally having been distinct. It's a glorious synaesthetic operetta (Hughes can be extremely funny) made from his sympathetic crackle to the crackle of the place. With his living phrasing, his imaginative connections, even his spiny dashes and asterisks, he fuses things together and himself with them, and causes the thorns of strangeness to flow, and then to sing.

RUTH FAINLIGHT
'To Be Harry'

———

Whatever you hung onto it has all
Abandoned you, quite faithless. Nothing has changed.

Even your poems – careless of how you died
They will now take up a strenuous career.
(The true book of your silence was buried with you.)
They will have the suspect air
Of talkative survivors –
They will tell all that happened, and more, except
How, in your worst moments, they failed you, and
   forsook you.

One thing has changed. Though it tries not to change.
The space inside our heads – the theatre
Where for a whole day you were surely happy
As the corpse of Oz,
Under flowers, sunk in a coffin, alive,
Round and round on the Circle Line, to music –
This has changed.

Everything has stopped. It is dark.
The audience has left.
Your great eye, unchanged
(Narcissus, inverted in his pool),
Goes on rehearsing, alone,
That last curtain of your last moment –

Lying in a garden, alone,
Eyelids apart, alive, the last moment,
Noticing leaves – then eyelids closing together –

Trying to get it right, just how it felt

Ted Hughes sent me this poem when I was editing my brother's until then uncollected work, a few years after his death, for a *Selected Poems* which was published in 1986. I do not know if Hughes included it in any subsequent collection of his own poems. Typing it for this piece it still moves me, still seems almost unbearably accurate in its comprehension of Harry, as if an act of shamanistic identification had taken place, as if Ted had slipped into the mind and into the skin of the dying man like an Aztec priest into the flayed skin of a sacrificial victim. In this case, the god to whom the sacrifice was made is without doubt the god of poetry.

A few details are necessary as explanatory notes to the poem. Harry died alone outside his isolated Welsh cottage, and the body was not found for some days. The title of the only publication in his lifetime, a pamphlet of poems, is *Sussicran* (Narcissus spelled backwards). He participated in a 'happening' in which his role was to be the body in a coffin carried into the Underground, and spent several hours travelling around the Circle Line with a cortege of excited mourners.

Harry and Ted were undergraduates at the same Cambridge College, Pembroke. I believe they met in the town, but as far as I know, because of the few years' difference in age, Ted had already left the college when Harry arrived. I met Ted in London, but not through my brother, and the friendship which began in 1961 continued through all the events and years that followed. Until he mentioned Harry's irregular, but persistent, appearances at his house in Devon, I had not been aware of the continuing attachment, nor how obsessed Harry was by the contrast between his own obscurity and Ted's success.

A hint was enough to evoke those meetings: Harry charming at first and then, as the strain told, becoming more and more

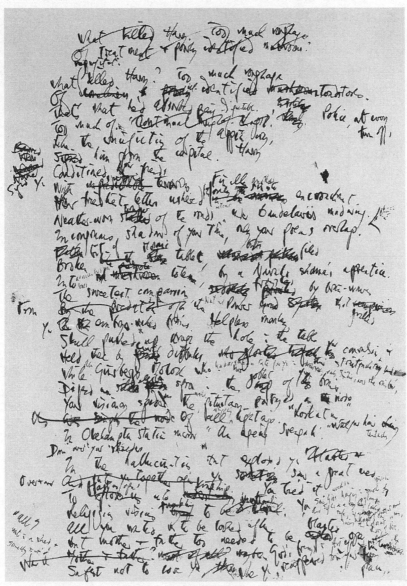

Manuscript of poem for Harry Fainlight from the collection of Roy Davids.
Not to be further reproduced without permission of Roy Davids.

aggressive and accusatory; the one towards whom these contra-dictory emotions were directed forced to be as neutral, patient and tolerant as possible. Knowing how difficult this often was for me, I shrank from the thought of what it might be like for Ted. Now, as well as the usual reaction of protective defensiveness concerning my brother, the knowledge of a shared experience and a sense of gratitude made me feel even closer to Ted.

This complex connection, as well as my great admiration for him as a poet, make me happy to add my voice to this tribute and memorial for an extraordinary man.

PART TWO

Poems for Ted Hughes

——

CHARLES CAUSLEY

In a Junior School

When I asked
What the poet did, a girl said,
'Make up true stories
Of people and animals
In his head.'

When I told them
He was also a farmer,
They said they thought
Farmers didn't have time to write
Stories and poems.

'He was born,' I said, 'in
Mytholmroyd in Yorkshire.'
'Myth . . . Myth . . . Mytholm . . .
Sounds like a hive of little bees,'
Somebody said.

'He still speaks,' I said,
'With the voice of his home-town.
Yorkshire people can tell
Just where he's from.'
They thought that was good.

'Once,' I said, 'he took home
A wounded badger.
Nursed it well, then set it free.'
All the children smiled;
Clapped their hands very loudly.

We listened to a poem and a story.
After the bell, they surged
Out of the classroom,
Some still murmuring, 'Myth . . .
Myth . . . Mytholm . . .' And laughing.

A boy turned to me. 'Poet and farmer!
Sounds good. Which is harder?'
I said, 'What would you say?'
'I'll let you know,' he said.
Went his way.

GILLIAN CLARKE

The Fisherman

From his pool of light in the crowded room, alone,
the poet reads to us. The sun slinks off
over darkening fields, and the moon is a stone
rolled and tumbled in the river's grief.

In a revolving stillness at the edge
of turbulent waters, the salmon hangs its ghost
in amber. On the shore of the white page
the fisherman waits. His line is cast.

The house is quiet. Under its thatch
it is used to listening. It's all ears
for the singing line out-reeled from his touch
till the word rises with its fin of fire.

A tremor in the voice betrays a hand
held tense above the surface of that river,
patient at the deep waters of the mind
for a haul of dangerous silver,

till electricity's earthed, and, hand on heart,
the line that arcs from air to shore is Art.

ROY DAVIDS

Memories, Reflections, Gratitudes (November 1998)

———

For Carol

Levelling the air out with his hand,
his huge handsome head held low,
watching me caught in the spiral of words,
living again his own first thrill,
bringing out the marvel of it all.
It was the way he made things magical.
Partly by his childlike sense;
his boyish charged excitedness.
As in our two days at the zoo
when he made a tiger snarl,
paid court to a cockatoo,
and was a gibbon gibbon.
That great roar of laughter,
like his cry for Ka and Golding,
rippling round the rafters.
The way he ruminated over food,
as if an antique mystic thought
passed over in some foreign fare.
Or watching, from his own armchair,
him rewriting Ovid on his knee,
the words just running from his pen,
under the half dim table light,
while we buffooned upon the floor.

Or as he simply sat and read,
rubbing his shingled eye.
Later, out on a walk with him,
falling in with his rise and fall;
it was the way he moved the mud
to let trapped water out to play.
Or, set a subject, as we set out,
With what mastery he wrought it,
endlessly engaging and engaged.
Then, those long drifting drives round Devon,
sometimes at a funeral pace,
reading new poems while he drove along,
questioning what this or that one meant.
We sketched out thirty books and schemes,
testing titles, shouting down the wind,
and piled the dirt on poets, politicians, friends.
He showed me all his ancient haunts,
and his folks me, in Devon and in York,
including the great Aunt Hilda,
and, in time, to most of those he knew
promoting me as agent and as friend.
Then there was his quite distinctive style
of leaning over bridges
to see how high the water was,
half turned, one foot just off the ground,
pointing at the fish I could not see.
And that day of mackerel and bream
when the pressure fell below the graph –
and, only just, we got inside the bar.
Calling, merely for a chat. 'What's new?
What's happened? Who's with who?'
or a thin message on the answer phone:
'It's only Ted; how are you?
I'll try the other line.'
Oh, we put the world to rights,
ripped up some reputations

and launched high gossip in the air.
Unnumbered rides to restaurants;
police-slow drives, to music, home;
the joy of quaffing rich men's wine,
revelling in the sheer indulgence of it all.
Three muscateers: Carol, Ted and me,
raising a glass to luck, and love, and us.
Late mornings; he was always late for meals.
Then our plans for merchant ventures,
him flirting with ideas, new explanations,
History was for living, not to learn,
scholars could keep the record right,
Magic's in a seance, saga, eagles' flight.
And yet how much his history was him.
One secret was the way he'd concentrate,
that word so early – adverbially –
in the famous fox he thought,
seeking the inmost spirit of each thing.
His will to share his world; to teach,
to open up horizons,
making them what you most desired;
like being converted at your own front door.
He opened up so many things for me,
taught me how to train my mind,
and even how to fall asleep.
How wonderful the memories are
of all the pleasures that we shared:
of the bowl of light we once raised high upon a Devon hill;
or the angel that did truly fly on a wall in Gloucestershire.
The mighty hand that clasped electric when we met or went,
and his big slow bull-like turn back into home,
captured in my mirror as I inched out of the lane.
Grateful also for your pheremonal smell;
for wild outbursts (letting off your steam);
for being so entirely free with me.
I loved your love of silence

and of the dusk and dawn;
your bible bond with Nature
and the sacred drama of the earth.
Your lion's eye,
the hare bone in your ear,
the crush and crashing of the bear.
Your vast capacious mind,
that temple of your inner life;
as visionary, your cell.
The depth of your response,
your heightened sense,
your tact,
your quite especial care.
The momentary jealousies;
the human flare.
And then your deep forgiveness.
For fishing; though I failed.
For having seen you cast
like Merlin laying on a spell.
For your passionate dispassion,
your sympathy; your courage;
your compassion.
For your legend'ry discretion,
and for the times you let me in.
Thank you for your fears about the world
and your dedication to yourself;
for your balance of perfection,
and powerful pursuit of it. For the thrill
of hearing that I'd done a good thing well.
I learned your sense of right and wrong
and felt you wait for me to grow aware.
I am in awe of your Shakespearean mind,
the great arc of your intellect,
your god-like talent and your skill,
the mellow music of your tongue;
your wisdom and your love of life,

your way with words in poems and in prose,
your insight and imagining.
The letters that lit up my days;
poems that made my mind fly free;
prose that forced the bended knee.
You were a purpose in my life;
a solid rock of reference;
still yet a presence in your empty chair.
You were loaned out by the gods,
retained their epic view
to see the cosmic broadbrush myth
and make mere men rejoice
at the complex complicatedness
of the spirit and the mind.
You were a seer, shaman, friend;
Coleridge-cum-Wordsworth, and yourself.
A loss to Art, you have diminished life
for those you leave bereft behind.
But it is one function of the great
to force on us the contradiction
of whether more to celebrate the work
or lament the life's extinction.
For now, I'll touch on simple benefactions,
on favours unconditionally done,
on comradeship and love assumed,
on your kindness, and for being shy.
And most perhaps for letting me be there,
and being so uniquely mine,
as in other ways, each quite unique,
you touched the lives of many men,
bringing out the best in them.
Your friendship was a miracle to me.
I really cannot comprehend
all that mighty heart is lying still.

MEDBH MCGUCKIAN

Shannon's Recovery

———

Moon-plunge
into the still river-like
womb-opening.

Father with your smooth lip
my graveless departure,
swallow its stillness.

Curve south, dearly matched
road that crossed
miles of my heart.

Be the three-way loved one
gone, a branch remembered
for its tugging shade,

its pencil-faint patches
drawing small frames
in a silver direction.

Touch me on every side,
sides of the living mountain,
my middle name in width.

And welcome back
ourselves, our own almost,
the coldness of my mouth now.

[189]

W. S. MERWIN

Planh for the Death of Ted Hughes

There were so many streets then in London
they were always going to be there
there were more than enough to go all the way
there were so many days to walk through them
we would be back with the time of year
just as we were in the open day

there were so many words as we went on walking
sometimes three of us sometimes two
half the sentences flying unfinished
as we turned up the collars that had been through the wars
autumn in the park spring on the hill
winter on the bridges under what we started to say

there was so much dew even in Boston
even in the bright fall so many planets poised
on the sills of transparent houses it was coming to pass
around us the whole time before it happened
before the hearts stopped one after the other
and the silent wailing began that would not end

we were going to catch up with some of the sentences
in France or Idaho we were going
to shake them out again and listen
to what had not been caught by history or geography

or touched at all by the venomous weather
it was only a question of where and when

Nine Ways of Looking at Ted Hughes

―――

Poet At Work

There he stands
a grizzly bear in a waterfall
catching the leaping salmon
in his scoopy paws

Full Moon And Little Frieda

little Frieda's life
will always be lit by that poem
and so will the life of the moon

Footwear Notes

bloody great clogs
carved out of logs
are the indoor shoes
of Ted Hughes

Not Cricket

Ted backsomersaulted to catch the meteorite lefthanded,
Rubbed it thoughtfully on the green groin of his flannels
And span it through the ribcage of the Reaper,
Whose bails caught fire

And jumped around the pitch like fire-crackers.
Said the commentator:
Yes Fred, it might have been a meteor –
Could have been a metaphor.

Rugby News

When Ted played front row forward
for Mytholmroyd Legendary RFC
his scrum strolled right through the walls
of Sellafield and out again the other side
like a luminous lava-flow

Out Of Focus

When you take a photograph of Ted
It's a job to get him all in –
like taking a snapshot of Mount Everest

Gastronomica

A large Mayakovsky
Or Ginsberg and tonic before the meal
Dry white Stevie Smith with the mousse of moose
Roast beef and Yorkshire pudding with a deep red Ted
Vintage Keats with the trifle
A glass of Baudelaire goes well with cheese
But afterwards
A bottomless goblet of Shakespeare's port
Or the blazing brandy of Blake

Fish-Eye

Said the Shark at the Sub-Aquatic Angling Contest
I caught an enormous Elizabeth Bishop the other day.
That's nothing, said the Whale,
I hooked a Ted Hughes, but he got away.

Ted-Watching

I saw him in his apeskin coracle
On the Paleolithic Swamp
He was chanting in a voice like limestone
To the rhythm of a dinosaur stomp

Then I saw him stalking barefoot
Over hills of stabbing gorse
And I knew he would never stop travelling
Till he reached the river's source

Next I saw him riding a mammoth
Near the banks of the holy stream
And I saw them stop to swim in a pool
Where silver birches dream

And the last I saw was his silhouette
Black against the Northern Lights
So I guess he's up there with the eagles
Who circle the golden heights.

Now the Pterodactyls may mock him
As he howls a prehistoric blues
But we know that he's a marvellous animal
And a great poet – Ted Hughes.

These were written while Ted was alive to celebrate his work and
make him smile that wonderful, lop-sided smile.

Now I would only like to add the following poem, especially for his family.

For Carol and Ted Hughes

Ophelia drowned
again and again
in the ice-crashing river
of Hamlet's brain;

but the weathercock whirled,
the river grew calmer
flowing through meadows
Of deep green summer.

Thank you, Carol,
bride of the son of Shakespeare,
Ted's gentle laughtergiver,
his newfound life,
his farm, his calm,
his beloved, his Devon
and his silver river.

PAUL MULDOON

Herm

He stands in under the hedge, among the sweet-smelling flags,
and holds out a white flag
to the distant plow-team
that makes directly for him through the teem

of rain, his head one of those plastered, round stones
atop a heap of pavers and kidney-stones.
Or he might be a young holly or ash
what with his brow-beat of ash.

As the team bears down on him through the fertile
meadow, the white on the lead horse's forehead (like the white
    where a tile
once fell off the wall behind the range)
comes into range

and a priest with a handkerchief
reels among those mown down in Derry, whispering to him,
    'Chief . . .'
as he grips his wrist and starts counting,
'We were counting

on you to hold steady, to stay
our consolation and stay.'
'But I've always taken my bearings from *you*' he'll hear himself
    remark,
'It was you I took for my mark.'

LES MURRAY

A Deployment of Fashion

In Australia, a lone woman
is being crucified by the Press
at any given moment.

With no unedited right
of reply, she is cast out
into Aboriginal space.

It's always for a defect in weeping:
she hasn't wept on cue
or she won't weep correctly.

There's a moment when the sharks are
still butting her, testing her protection,
when the Labor Party, or influence,

can still save her. Not the Church,
not other parties. Even at that stage
few men can rescue her.

Then she goes down, overwhelmed
In the feasting grins of pressmen,
and Press women who've moved

from being owned by men
to being owned by fashion,
these are more deeply merciless.

She is rogue property,
she must be taught her weeping.
It is done for the millions.

Sometimes the millions join in
with jokes: how to get a baby
in the Northern Territory? Just stick

your finger down a dingo's throat.
Most times, though, the millions
stay money, and the jokes

are snobbish media jokes:
Chemidenko. The Oxleymoron.
Spittle, like the flies on Black Mary.

After the feeding frenzy
sometimes a ruefully balanced last lick
precedes the next selection.

I only once saw at first hand part of Ted Hughes's long torment at
the hands of militants. This was at the awful Adelaide Festival of
1976, and I mentioned it at the time in an essay. Many of his fellow
poets will have seen more of his suffering, and yet I'm not aware of
any major defences of him, in verse anyway, by his British
colleagues. I apologize for any I may have missed. The enervating
cliché that 'poetry makes nothing happen' has perhaps held us in
thrall as effectively as the fear of being singled out ourselves. The
poem above doesn't of course refer to the Hughes case, but to
something vaster and more concerted, if also more childishly brief
each time around. It began as a recurrent media device in Australia
with the Chamberlain Dingo-Baby case in the late 1970s, and on
its first try-out caused the imprisonment of a totally innocent
woman. Other victims followed at quickening intervals. When I
published this poem in *The Australian* in October 1997, the
savagery it describes came to an abrupt halt, and it has not
recommenced at anything like its former strength. Women
journalists seem to have heeded the admonition.

I sometimes wonder, in activist moments of my own, whether concerted deployment of fashion against individuals should not be outlawed, perhaps by a strong United Nations convention that might appropriately bear Ted Hughes's name. I'd like to see that: malign political bullying in the manner of the schoolyard brought up short by the Hughes Convention. It would be a worthy memorial to so individual and uncollective a poet.

WILLIAM SCAMMELL

Goa

Since there is no elephant
or Mercedes to be had
the family is abroad
on a Vespa, all five of them
rippling through the early dark,
mother and baby whispering along
sidesaddle on the back.

*

There the banyan tree drops down aerial
roots, enlarges itself in creepers,
making a temple of its own limbs,
a hanging garden, a torrent of suggestions;
plumps up space the way a dancer does,
the way a sitar plucks notes out of its belly
and hugs them, not sure where sorrow ends
and the rest of the world begins.

*

A trumpet sounds at the hotel gates
and there stands Ganesh himself
taller than you'd ever imagined,
parked up on his legs, fronting
the cameras, eyes lost and whalish

in that round head, dumb as the flames
they broke him with, which blacken
the pillars of my chest.

*

In the paddy fields they put and take
all day, bent over the eye of the needle
that stitches them to earth, warm hungry mud,
the long field path, the goodness of God.

*

Inflorescence of a Matisse
languorous on cerulean blue:
the bay as a hedonist masterpiece.
The palms have nothing to say to this.
Why should they? Beauty is all ours.
They lean upwards, as the law insists,
watching the ocean mop its muddy floors.

*

The lads go on hammering long poles
into sand, weaving their shady roofs
out of such handy materials
as the spiky, biodegradable leaves

of the spirit, recommended by gurus
everywhere, lest we think we are gods,
renting the sahib his sunbed and pillows
or selling him soapstone bits and bobs.

These are the one-off cafés, built each year
in a couple of days by quick and practised hands
to service the restless boulevardier
walking his cut-out shadow across the sands.

They riffle off notes with the head of Gandhi
bent over the spindle of his wheel,

all wire-rim specs, and self-sufficiency,
the ghost of that non-violent smile.

*

The fingers are drumming, drumming
under those exquisite rāgs,
the heel of the hand for thunder
rained down by unforgiving gods.

Gold for the gipsy women, gold and silk
riotous against their oily black
hair and skin, done up as slaves
to mock the slavery of wives.

CHARLES TOMLINSON

For T. H.

━━━━━

I caught today something that you'd once said.
It re-formed in the echo-chambers of the head
Bringing with it the voice of its saying
(Your voice) and even the atmosphere of a morning
On Hartland's cliffs and the steady pace that we
Kept up beside the murmurings of that sea.
It was the music of speech you were describing
And the way such sounds must either die or sing,
The satisfactions of speech being musical
When we talk together: a man with no talent at all
For music in the matters of everyday
Stays tedious despite what he has to say –
Even on subjects that might wake one's fantasies,
For what we want is that exchange of melodies,
The stimulation of tunes that answer one another
In the salt and sway of the sea's own weather
As they did that day we faced into the wind there,
And now return in thought, so that I hear
The dance of the words, like verse itself, renew
The sounded lineaments of the world we move through.

PART THREE

On Ted Hughes

A. ALVAREZ

Ted Hughes

——

I first met Ted Hughes in the spring of 1960, just after the publication of his second book, *Lupercal*. I was then in the middle of what turned out to be ten years as poetry critic and editor of *The Observer* and *Lupercal* struck me as the best book by an English poet that I had read since I started my stint. When I wrote a piece to say so, the paper asked me to interview him. He and Sylvia Plath and their baby daughter Frieda were living in a tiny flat in Chalcot Square in London, and I was living near Swiss Cottage, so we agreed to take our children for a walk on Primrose Hill, the no-man's land that lay between.

Even then, when he was just beginning, Ted was a powerful presence. He reminded me of Heathcliff – also a Yorkshireman – big-boned and brooding, with dark hair flopping forward over his craggy face, watchful eyes and an unexpectedly witty mouth. He was a man who seemed to carry his own climate with him, to create his own atmosphere, and in those days that atmosphere was all black. It was a darkness that many women seemed to find irresistible: one said, 'He looks like a gunfighter, like Jack Palance in *Shane*'; according to another, even more awe-struck, 'He looks like God would look if you got there'. Hughes himself seemed not to care about his appearance. His clothes were worn and shapeless and his guiding principle for choosing them was Henry Ford's 'any colour as long as it's black': black corduroy jacket, black trousers, black shoes and socks. Later, Sylvia Plath metamorphosed him into 'a man in black with a Meinkampf look / And a love of the rack and the screw', but in those days, when Existentialism was the fashion, black was the uniform of chic young intellectuals. It went with spouting Sartre and Camus and smoking Gauloises.

Hughes was nothing like the would-be Marxist-Existentialists who hung around London's new coffee shops, but he also didn't have much in common with the Movement poets who saw the world as a Lowry painting – a long provincial perspective populated by gloomy stick figures – and wrote poems like well-turned essays, with a beginning, a middle, and a moral at the end. Hughes was more self-assured, a man who knew where he was coming from, solidly based, and in the world he inhabited wild animals figured a great deal more prominently than people.

That, too, was nothing new in the 1950s, when F. R. Leavis and his acolytes ruled the roost in English Departments and D. H. Lawrence was a cult figure for the literary young. According to Leavis, Lawrence was the greatest artist in the Great Tradition because, among other reasons, he was the last writer whose roots were in an England that had not yet been ruined by the industrial revolution. In dingy, pinched, unheated postwar Britain that wasn't an argument which had much appeal for anyone who had had the luck to cross the Atlantic and see what the industrial revolution could do to make life easy and comfortable. So we concentrated on Lawrence's feeling for nature and his loving descriptions of it. Even a city boy like me knew – or pretended to know – about birds, beasts and flowers because Lawrence had written about them so seductively.

Like Lawrence's, Ted's background was northern and working-class and he was profoundly influenced by Lawrence's writings, although his take on them was very much his own. It was Lawrence without the nerves and the preaching, but also without the flowers and the tenderness. Lawrence's creatures – the snake, the mountain lion and tortoises, the stallion St Mawr, even the mosquito – were like the people in his novels: he was always in a dialogue with them, using them to voice his preoccupations and letting them argue back vehemently. Hughes's creatures – the hawk, the otter, the fox, the pike – were different. They were hunters and the hunted, irredeemably alien, and it was their otherness that interested him most: their wildness, their world of instincts and threat and incipient violence, a world in which even thrushes are killers and flowers are rooted in nightmares. When Hughes set out 'To Paint A Water Lily' the flower he came up with was nothing like the ones Monet painted at Giverny. It was suspended between horror and horror, between an air shimmering with murderous insects and the pond's bed where 'Prehistoric bedragonned times / Crawl that darkness with Latin names.' In the domain of Hughes's unforgiving imagination, beauty existed but always perilously, as an act of will, and the forces ranged against it were terrible. Wild creatures, for him, were like dreams; they were his way through to hidden parts of his mind.

He had read English when he went up to Cambridge, then switched to anthropology. He switched because of a dream which he told me soon after we first met, wryly, almost as a joke against himself. He was labouring late at night, he said, on his weekly essay – I think it was about Dr Johnson – bored by it and getting nowhere. Finally, he gave up and went to bed. That night he dreamed a fox came into his college room, went over to his desk, peered at the unfinished essay and shook its head in disgust. Then it placed a paw on the scribbled pages and they burst into flame. The next day, Hughes wrote a poem about the dream – 'The Thought-Fox' – and left it on his desk when he went to bed. The same night the dream-fox was back. It read the poem, nodded approvingly and gave the sleeping poet a genial thumbs-up. Hughes took the visitation as a sign: the academic study of literature wasn't for him; it was time to change his life as well as his degree course. Anthropology may not altogether have been what he was after, but at least it concerned itself with more primitive and instinctual societies than our own.

What is most important about this story is that the dream came when he needed it and he was able to listen to what it was telling him. And this is what set Hughes apart from most young poets of his generation, even from Sylvia Plath when they first met: he seemed to have easy, immediate access to his sources of inspiration, a permanently open hotline to his unconscious.

Later, when Hughes told his story of the dream-fox to Professor John Carey, an eminently sane and sensible witness, he had translated it into something Jungian and more portentous: the fox was another persona – Hughes with a fox's head. But it doesn't matter that the wild animals went with a belief in mysteries and the under-life and black magic, or that he increasingly used what I thought was mumbo-jumbo to get where he wanted to be – astrology, hypnosis, ouija boards, or the dottier forms of Jungian magical thinking. (Jung, like Hughes, was a country boy fallen among intellectuals.) All that mattered was that the poems he fished out of the depths were shimmering with life.

He kept his beliefs strictly to himself, even back then when we were all young and shooting our mouths off at any old bright idea that had come along that week. I remember him as quiet-spoken, witty, shrewd and modest. He was not a man to give himself airs and he never came on as a poet. It was not a line of work that would have cut much ice with his neighbours in Yorkshire or Devon, and he had no taste for the literary world. But he was utterly sure of his talent and you could never predict what he would say; his reactions to everything – to people, places, books – were always his own.

Like every prolific poet, Hughes published his share of poems that merely go through the motions, poems that might have been written by another of his dream premonitions, the 'Famous Poet' he savaged in his arrogant youth. But even when his duties as Poet Laureate seemed to have got the better of him, he never lost his genius for the muscle and sinew of the language, and he saved some of his finest work for the end. *Birthday Letters* was his version of his troubled marriage to Sylvia Plath. Up until then, Hughes had doggedly refused to talk about Plath or to respond to the wild accusations of treachery by feminists who hacked his name off her gravestone or turned up at his readings with placards calling him murderer. I assume he decided to set the record straight only when he knew he was dying, rather than leave the manuscripts for biographers and academics to pick over and sensationalize.

The poems don't try to soften her violent rages or blur her crippling fears or make their life together seem other than a crazy highwire act – one slip and they were in the abyss – but they bring her startlingly back to life, often in a style that sounds curiously like hers: tightly controlled despite their apparently free form, packed with images, fast-talking and full of foreboding. They are the most vulnerable he ever wrote and also the saddest: all that love and talent gone to waste, her death, his grief. The book is a kind of funeral monument to them both.

Over the years, I have met dozens, maybe hundreds of people who called themselves poets. Some were published, a few were famous, many were – and still are – unknown. But Hughes was one of the few who had an authentic voice like no one else's, a voice that comes out of nowhere and is always unexpected. He belongs up there with the other true poets of this half century whom I've been lucky to know: Zbigniew Herbert, Robert Lowell, John Berryman, Miroslav Holub and, of course, Sylvia Plath.

YEHUDA AMICHAI
Ted Hughes's Poetry

—————

I am not an academic, nor a professional critic. I was a friend and a fellow poet of Ted Hughes. I would like to suggest three metaphors for Ted's whole work rather than pick out a single poem.

Hughes's work is a landscape. I live in a region where, unlike in the English landscape, three kinds of hills can be clearly recognized because they are not covered with lush greenery. There are the geologically old hills, there are much younger volcano-shaped hills and there are the Tels. The Tel is a mound with layers of human settlement and culture one on top of the other. These layers tell the stories of happiness and fire, of war and peace. Each layer also used pieces of earlier destruction for their own. Hughes's poems are all like these hills. They are a whole landscape. I would go as far as to say that each poem is a hill; ancient geological, covered with plants and volcanic, and archaeological-layered all together. Deep down there is still a potency of volcanic action in each poem, which at any time can burst through all the layers. This is the basic energy in his work, still latent. But out of this, also, sometimes, a clearwater spring emerges.

The second metaphor would describe Hughes's opus as one huge symphony. Sometimes chaotic, sometimes harmonic with solo voices, of humans and of animals; sometimes humans with animal voices, sometimes animals with human voices.

The third metaphor would compare the work of Hughes to a large hidden valley. We can't see it but we can hear the voices, sometimes sad, sometimes harsh and sometimes happy. We are dependent on the wind, turning around and around, and bringing us pieces and glimpses of the multitude of goings-on in Hughes's valley.

Above all Hughes's poetry is both piercing and sometimes cruel; it is healing and it brings comfort to our own lives.

With Ted Hughes

The late John L. (Jack) Sweeney was the first person to encourage seriously my efforts to paint. He was, I believe, also the first to record Ted Hughes's poetry. Sweeney visited County Clare each summer. Then, and shortly after *The Hawk in the Rain* was published, he gave me a record Ted had made for his Poetry Room at Harvard, and said that as we were both countrymen and absorbed by the life of animals, we should meet. He also said we shared a fascination with violence, something I remember violently repudiating.

Ted and I corresponded. We met, I am pretty sure, in 1958 or 1959 in London where Ted and Sylvia had a small flat (loaned to them I think by the Merwins). We spent a fascinating afternoon at the Regent's Park Zoo where I remember an Andean wolf pacing its cage while we both watched in silence. Later I wrote to him with a sense of gleeful one-upmanship that I had been allowed to watch tigers mate at the Dublin Zoo – an astonishing episode seen by very few. We met next in County Clare in The Burren near where I lived, and one evening we lay on our backs hidden in slots of rocks watching wild geese fly off Sleive Na Maun to their watering ground.

After that, sharing a love for angling, we fished together in many places in Devon and in Ireland. I think especially of that time, before Ted's son Nick became a fishery biologist, when we all, obsessed with pike, made spring and autumn forays for the creature in lakes all over Ireland. Much later we made a set of lithographs together. 'The Great Irish Pike' was written, drawn, and printed in Devon in ten days. Ted's writing, his enormous gift of empathy for the wild in life has meant, over forty years, a very great deal to me.

TERRY GIFFORD

Ted Hughes and South Yorkshire: 'A Motorbike'

Ted Hughes wrote a book (*Remains of Elmet*) about the West Yorkshire landscape and culture in which he spent his first eight years and to which his family returned thirteen years later. But his South Yorkshire experience (at Mexborough from 13 September 1938 to 13 September 1951) is less identifiable behind the stories in *Wodwo* and scattered poems such as 'Her Husband', 'Esther's Tom Cat' and references in 'The Angel' and 'That Morning'. 'A Motorbike', however, is firmly located in Mexborough, but a South Yorkshire that represents the bleakness of postwar England. With some risk of hyperbole ('The foreman, the boss, was as bad as the SS') it does achieve some remarkable expressions of period ennui ('The shrunk-back war ached in their testicles'). To erupt into life too enthusiastically, however, as both motorcycle and motorcyclist do, is to risk death – in this case 'On the long straight west of Swinton', which remains an accident blackspot to this day.

In October 1997, when I was preparing to lead with David Sissons a 'Ted Hughes Literary Tour of South Yorkshire' for a Sheffield Literature Festival, I wrote to Hughes with a number of questions to which he responded fulsomely in a letter of 6 October 1997 from which all the following quotations come. (It seems in retrospect that he was putting on record some cherished biographical information.) So, on an appropriately misty morning, we were able to visit Hughes's Schofield Street Primary School (now boarded up) just across Mexborough's main street from the corner newsagent's shop run by his parents, now a furniture shop haunted, we were told, in the half that was occupied by the Hughes's neighbours. ('No we never heard of anything ghostly next door,' Hughes wrote. 'But I wouldn't be surprised if that family imprinted in the brickwork, joists, foundations, and space.')

Most of our time on our little tour was spent in the landscapes of the two farms on which the young Hughes escaped the privations of Mexborough and Old Denaby – 'once like the darkest badlands, narrow streets full of black miners and their wives'. Ted used to cross the river below Mexborough by ferry. 'The Ferryman was a little crippled fellow I never knew as anything but Limpy. He had a stone hut at the top of the ramp down to the ferry . . . heard some odd stories in that hut.'

Then Ted was in 'my kingdom':

I knew that land – the whole of Manor Farm . . . – better than any place I've ever known. I think I knew every inch. I had trap-lines of various kinds all over it. I crawled over most of it. I knew every rat-hole, let alone every rabbit-hole. From 1938 – when my brother discovered it delivering newspapers . . . – to 1944/45 when my big love affair with Crookhill Farm and the Wholey family began. (. . .) I'd turn in at Manor Farm . . . to inspect my traps (they began with a line of dozens of mouse traps all over the farm buildings: I used to sell the mouse skins at school) . . . During all the time I roamed over that ground I never met one other person strayed over from the town . . . And that was through the war years when a rabbit was a desirable object, and a partridge precious. There were always plenty of rabbits, partridges in every field pretty well, and a few hares. When I went back there in 1982 for my old English teacher's funeral, the entire farm was one field, the copses had been ploughed out along with the hedges. Even the quarry had been smoothed over and ploughed as required . . . A year or two ago I went back to the farm-house itself and got one of the devastating shocks of my life.

Manor Farm is now a huge pub with historic faded photographs of the old farm in the entrance. Crookhill Farm, to which Ted's allegiance transferred through his friendship with his 'pal' John Wholey ('John was as obsessed by guns and fishing as I was'), is now a golf course. We risked death between the greens to visit a small pond which was one candidate for the source of the poem 'Pike'. Hughes had commented: 'The pond of my pike poem is still a classified secret, though we did catch pike in quite a few places. There were big pike in that tiny pond at Crookhill. Another bit of soul-damage there, last time I saw that.'

A much more likely candidate for the pike pond is the bigger, lily-padded pond at Roche Abbey close by, 'whose lilies and muscular tench / Had outlasted every visible stone / Of the monastery that planted them'.

When, as Hughes wrote in 'A Motorbike', 'England had shrunk to the size of a dog-track', he himself was not 'working up a life out of the avenues / And the holiday resorts and the dance-halls', but accumulating the deep knowledge and values that would make him a laureate of nature, a spokesman for an alternative healing way of life in intimate, if problematic, connection with our home, the earth. This is the legacy that Ted Hughes has left us, a true way of finding a source of vitality that the motorcyclist seeks, but which reconnects our inner nature with that outer nature in which we live and have abused so much. The growing consumer society of 'A Motorbike' and the mechanized thrill of escape can now be seen as a metaphor for our self-destructive postwar society.

Hughes was glad to hear that salmon were returning to the river Don in South Yorkshire: 'In those days The Don seemed to me more or less solid chemicals – bubbling, fuming, multi-coloured.' Perhaps some things have changed for the better in South Yorkshire, although the jury is clearly still out on the global question and that of our species as a whole.

MIROSLAV HOLUB

Ted Hughes in Czech

Ted Hughes was first presented to Czech readers through a fine translation by Stanislav Mares in the magazine *Svetova literatura* (World Literature) in 1966. It was a selection from *The Hawk in the Rain* and *Lupercal*, introduced with a thorough theoretic study. My feeling was: at last, here is a real man, not a poetic impostor, a real man with an astonishingly vigorous imagination and drive. I started to read Ted Hughes in the original.

Then came *Modern Poetry in Translation* (edited by Hughes and Daniel Weissbort) where Czech poetry had an important role. It seemed in the 1960s, the period of revival of our culture and temporary liberation of public life, that at least some of us shared something with Ted Hughes, such as his attitude to cruelty, to 'poetry after Auschwitz' and his viewing of 'Man' from the point of view of 'Non-Man', his inclination to some sort of 'neolithic surrealism' (as opposed to literary surrealism), his immanent protest against the 'official culture'. Just emerging from the 'disaster-centre of the modern world' (Hughes in the introduction to Pilinszky) we were reinforced in the feeling or opinion that poetry means something and leads somewhere, provided it has enough energy.

I met Ted Hughes only twice in person, in London and in Cambridge, but I have the feeling I meet him whenever I write a poem. I wouldn't have his inclinations to Eastern myths, for I am just a scientist with my own batch of darkness and reassurance but – since *Crow* – I was and still am convinced that a poem must be a drama, a report from a battle; that the poem must have blood (and not just juices, words and postcard images): 'Crow gazed after the bounding hare / Speechless with admiration' after the hare has eaten Crow's hunting, well-trained words.

From time to time I remember a war incident near my native town: people escaping from a train which is being attacked by fighter planes; they are machine gunned, running down a slope; a boy's leg is cut off by bullets at the shin, but he keeps running, only the stump of his leg sinks with each step deeper and deeper into the grass. Crow: 'The bullets pursued their curses / Through clods of stone, earth and skin / Through intestines, pocket-books, brain, hair, teeth / According to Universal laws / And mouths cried "Mamma". . .'

In the early 1980s I wrote the poem 'Princesses': '. . . in bedrooms behind closed curtains: / the happy decapitation of princesses. // Their bodies are taken / hostage . . . / And in the morning, naked in the nakedness / of the other person, / we ask, whose hands are these // and which play was it / that had this immortal scene / from the Dynasty of If.' Rereading Hughes's 'Lovesong', I realize now that my poem is a typical case of 'intuition', that is remembering again what we have meanwhile forgotten. The forgotten has become a part of ourselves, proving the full histocompatibility between the two poems and poets.

It was a real joy to discover in 1986 that poems from *Wodwo*, *Crow* and *Cave Birds* had finally appeared in Prague in a Czech edition, *Jeskynni ptaci* (Cave Birds) translated by Jaroslav Koran, and that it is the strongest book of poetry of the era. (It was the time when people waited in queues for newly released books, including poetry, not only because of the presence of totalitarian Black Beasts, but also because some people really needed poetry and others imitated them.)

In my view Koran's translation was superb – it was a real Ted Hughes. Very few English and American poets were so well served; it was another case of histocompatibility.

Koran has even found a special Czech word for Crow. The

crow in Czech is feminine, but Hughes/Koran's crow is masculine, like the Czech rook. This 'he crow' is a Crowego, a Crowcolour, a King of Carrion, a myth already at the word level.

Since this Czech book I can't resist the feeling that Ted Hughes became part of the Czech context, at least of a robust and struggling Czech poetry, like that of the late Holan and of our 'angry poet' Ivan Divis. I didn't find anybody who was as aware of Hughes's influence as I was. But something Crow-like was also in our atmosphere.

A new book is in preparation. Under the title *Nocni tance* (Night Dances), it will be an interesting confrontation of poems by Ted Hughes and Sylvia Plath, in translations by Tomas Hrach.

Hughes, who was so devoted to the transfer and translation of poetry, deserves to be presented here at such different periods and especially now, when the Czech 'poetic paradigm' shifts towards something like lyrical minimalism and the withering away of all sense and meaning.

In my opinion, right now we need more of *Cave Birds*. We badly need poets who show that poetry is a little more than whining or purring and at the beginning (and at the end) there are no words, but an outcry.

Ted Hughes and the Calder Valley

I remember the day I discovered the poems of Ted Hughes in the vivid way people recall the death of Kennedy. The larger context of the time in which I fell upon 'Wind', 'October Dawn', 'Hawk Roosting', 'Esther's Tomcat', 'Otter' and 'Pike', is lost to me. It must have been during the early 1960s. I no longer know which edition of A. Alvarez's *The New Poetry* anthology they were in, for since purchasing it I have lost, given it away and replaced it several times. I was in my early twenties, a little late for someone with poetic ambitions to be discovering contemporary poetry, but such was the isolation in which I found myself. Poetry, like sex in youth, was an untutored atavism. But isolation has its rewards, for water tastes sweetest in the desert. I remember that I was playing truant from art college in Manchester, and with sketchbook and paints had cycled dreamily into Cheshire in search of my muse, but the remainder of that day is forgotten except for the moment in a Chester book shop when I fell into a trance over the anthology. Among Robert Lowell, R. S. Thomas, Larkin and Silkin, I homed in on the work of my namesake. I would bet that those early Hughes poems struck many a person in the same way at around that time.

It was in the *Guardian* I think that I read an interview in which Ted Hughes described his discovery of D. H. Lawrence as being like 'reading about my own life'. This was a feeling that I shared about both Lawrence and Hughes, because of the working class, northern England, especially the Pennine background, and because of the inspiration derived from the natural world, and from the muse's need to relate it to industrial desecration. My thrill from discovering these authors, as a light strung ahead of one along a dark tunnel, cannot have been a surprising nor an unusual one.

It is Ted Hughes's later work that makes him a particularly significant poet: his extension of the, in large part, too narrowly envisaged poetry of many of his contemporaries into a wider context by means of his self-created mythology. That is why for example I found him adulated in Soviet-run Czechoslovakia. There was indeed an occasional hardening of the arteries of his critical and other sensibilities in some of the later verse. What remains of most meaning to me have been his returns – as return he apparently had to – to the matter and manner, the vigour and keenness, of his earlier appraisals of the world, for example in *Moortown* and in parts of *Birthday Letters*.

My life and his had some curious correspondences following my early discovery. Happening, for utterly unconnected reasons, to live for twenty years only five miles from his birthplace, having the same surname and at an earlier stage of my work at any rate a related subject matter, resulted in some oddities. Even before I had published a first pamphlet collection, as I was apparently the only person in Halifax to order poetry books, the bookseller there asked me if I was 'Mr Hughes, the poet'. Not being prepared to say that I *wasn't* a poet, I was asked to sign a copy of *Lupercal,* which I did with, of course, my own name.

Later I received generosity and kindness from Hughes for which I will always be grateful. In particular, he wrote the most perceptive review of my first novel *Where I Used to Play on the Green.* The novel, concerning a self-tormented parson, was set during the eighteenth century in Ted Hughes's own area of West Yorkshire. Hughes pointed to what Keith Sagar elsewhere has called the *duende* of the West Yorkshire district – using Lorca's definition of this Spanish word, in his 1933 lecture. The balancing of the creative spirit on the ridge between life and death – to put it as simply as possible.

The antithesis is violently represented in West Yorkshire's Calder Valley, Ted Hughes's birthplace, by the juxtapositions of especially beautiful moorland with an industrial decline – the 'historical evidence' of a 'spiritual genocide' in 'the barren island bounded by Halifax, Todmorden, Colne and Keighley: the broken fragments of a cruel decalogue, tumbled about a giant graveyard.'

What interests me now is that, with hindsight, it seems to be what for me empowered poems about pike and hawk. And what it was that made it possible for Ted Hughes to raise the light of recognition in those un-English peoples who have recently rather than distantly suffered genocide and holocaust. '. . . the psychological atrocity . . . *the* national disaster . . . just how the spiritual concentration camp of the industrial revolution was created . . .' can become an obsession in West Yorkshire. Death and life lie juxtaposed.

The landscape forces the imagination to strive. As Ted Hughes described in 'Pennines in April':

through

Landscapes gliding blue as water
Those barrellings of strength are heaving slowly and heave
To your feet and surf upwards
In a still, fiery air, hauling the imagination,
Carrying the larks upward.

MICHAEL MORPURGO

Ted Hughes: Children's Champion

It was as a classroom teacher that I first read Ted Hughes's poetry, over thirty years ago. I was looking for poetry that would stimulate a bunch of apathetic adolescents, language that would sound so wonderful when I read it out loud, that it would hit the mark. They were at once wide-eyed with wonder. They even asked for an encore. So, I had roused them. Rather, Ted Hughes had roused them. The truth was, of course, that he had roused me.

Subsequently I devoured all of his work that I could find, and then came across a series of radio programmes he had written for 'Listening and Writing', a BBC schools programme, entitled *Poetry in the Making*. I doubt there has ever been written a more lucid, more enabling invitation to write. I was enthralled. So was my class. 'You see,' I told them, 'you can do it too. I can do it too. He says so, he's shown us how.'

I did it right. I didn't sit them down and just get them writing. We went to our local nature reserve. No clipboards, just eyes and ears and our own thoughts. I gave them time. They wrote, and I wrote with them. I spent my time stumbling through a forest of clichés. My head full of the sounds and sights and rhythms of Gerard Manley Hopkins and Dylan Thomas and of Ted Hughes himself. The children, with their fresher eye, wrote the most keenly observed, most original work they had ever done. What Ted Hughes had done for us, for all of us, was to enable us to believe we could do it, that we were not dolts, we were writers, all of us.

Twenty-five years later, when we came to live and work in deepest Devonshire, my wife and I found ourselves to be near neighbours of Ted Hughes. Down on the River Torridge at dusk, I met the man behind the poems. We were trying at the time to launch an educational charity which we called 'Farms for City Children', a project that would enable thousands of city children a year to come to live and work for a week on our farm. Unlike almost everyone else we told about this seemingly starry-eyed notion, Ted Hughes responded not just positively, but enthusiastically. He saw us through our growing pains, our failures, anxieties and follies. He came and read his poetry to the children in the evenings, and all the while he also encouraged my early fumbling attempts to become a writer, a teller of tales. He became President of 'Farms for City Children', and remained to the end of his life an unswerving source of support.

Now, very much thanks to him, there are now two more such 'Farms For City Children', one in Wales, and another in Gloucestershire. At Treginnis Isaf near St David's, as the young farmers troop off to work in the fields, they pass a plaque in the courtyard which reads:

> The animals and children of Treginnis
> Hushed by the sea and the sky
> Can hear a high gull cry
> God rides in the wind above Treginnis

> Ted Hughes

And at Wick Court, near Frampton on Severn, the children can look up from their own poetry-making in the Quiet Room and read this, etched in clay in Ted Hughes's own hand:

> Wick with its five wizard hats
> Wished in ghosts and prayed in bats
> Till out of the dried up well of thirst
> A fountain of new children burst

Then all Wick's memories trooped from sleep
Goats, ducks, chickens, cows, pigs, sheep.

Ted Hughes was indeed the most wonderful enabler. A source of extraordinary ideas himself, he would often latch on to the ideas of others and simply find a way to make them sing. One such notion in his last year of life was the creation of 'The Children's Laureate', an honour to be awarded biannually to a children's writer or illustrator to focus awareness of the best of children's books amongst adults and children alike, to raise its status, to celebrate it. He sat down and wrote letters, he enthused about it, endowed it with the serious rationale it needed, gave it life. Twelve months after the idea was first mooted to him Britain will have its first Children's Laureate.

Ted Hughes was indeed a children's champion. He touched young lives, making readers and writers of so many of us. He opened our eyes, he taught us to fly.

CHRISTOPHER REID

Ted Hughes as Reader

━━━━━

The poet's voice. I heard it first at Oxford, at the Union. It was the early 1970s. *Crow* was just out, very much the book of the moment, and the Debating Hall was jammed. But it was not a barnstorming performance, such as the circumstances and hype might have suggested. The stagy gothic hall, so used to the stridency and bellowing of the university's politicos and show-offs, this time heard something different. The drama of *Crow* itself was harsh and shocking, but the voice that conveyed it was mostly subdued. There was a tremble, a searching tentativeness, to it. It seemed as awed as we were. The poems were interspersed with prose narrative, bits of Crow's story omitted from the published text. Hearing them was like getting a secret glimpse into the workings of what had been powerful but also puzzling; we were being, not just diverted, but initiated, introduced to mysteries. It was a privilege to be there, and I suspect that anyone present who was at all touched felt it as his or her own unique piece of luck. My friend Craig Raine was in the audience with his mother-in-law Lydia Pasternak Slater, who went up to Ted Hughes afterwards and told him how much he reminded her of Mayakovsky. I had never seen or heard anyone like him, myself.

After a long gap, I was to hear Ted Hughes read publicly on several further occasions, and of course there were the tapes he made – of his own poetry and Eliot's, and of some of his children's books. If only he had done more in this line. There was, briefly, the notion of a series of educational videos, in which he would have talked directly to camera about Shakespeare and read from the plays and poems, but it never came about. Young audiences, children, minds as yet undamaged by bad education, were what he seemed to prefer. Nonetheless, if he were addressing, say, a room full of booksellers, as part of some marketing drive organized by his publisher, he would perform for them equally generously. Being a big man, he could stoop over a lectern and huddle himself around it in a way that suggested both protective concern for what was being read and, through the unguarded gap in front of him, an invitation to share it. It was instructive to learn, from professional dealings with him, how close his reading manner was to his style of conversation. The same measured tremolo was audible in both, and the same mid-sentence, or mid-phrase, catch of drawl implying thoughtfulness before a quick pounce on the right word. Volume was never necessary. Accuracy was what mattered. I heard more than once, at readings, the preamble to his great poem 'October Salmon'; a brief lecture, in effect, on the entire life-cycle of the fish, almost as vivid as the poem itself, and kept so each time by the oral storyteller's knack of spontaneity, his need and ability to reach the heart of the matter by ever-renewed stratagems. Once again, it was like listening to a spellbinding bedtime story.

Of course, we were not an audience of babies and we were not about to fall asleep. Nor were we being talked down to, nor sweetly tricked. Something else was going on. What Ted Hughes wanted, I believe, and what he came closer to achieving than any poet or actor I can think of, was that his voice should provide the most natural and expansive arena possible for the events of his poems. Not that it was a voice purged of personality. The arena in question had a highly distinctive, rugged and gritty texture to it, and a particularly hard, unsparing, tragic light was apt to fall across it. Musically and dramatically, though, it was designed to welcome listeners and to hold their attention. While terrible and frightening things happened there, it was not meant to scare us away. In fact, it was a good place to be.

A Poet and a Critic

I have published a great deal on Hughes's works elsewhere. I would like to use this opportunity for some more personal thoughts and recollections.

Close relationships between major poets and academic critics are hardly to be expected: a clear case of chalk and cheese. Yet I was lucky enough to have Ted Hughes's friendship, encouragement and inspiration for a quarter of a century.

Perhaps, however, I do myself an injustice by describing myself as an academic critic. As a tutor in adult education for the whole of my career, working from home, teaching largely Workers' Educational Association classes, I have had the best of both worlds – one foot in the academic world and one in the real world.

It has always seemed to me that the main task for the critic, perhaps the only valid task, is to try to become a more adequate reader. It is certainly not to pass judgements on literature; for critics, like the rest of us (including the writers themselves) are merely, in Hughes's words, 'criminals being judged by literature'. The writer himself is perhaps the arch-criminal, being judged by his own imagination. If he can correct or heal himself, bring himself closer to 'a proper knowledge of the sacred wholeness of nature, and a proper alignment of our behaviour within her laws', then the mysterious power of imaginative art can, given an adequate and open response, magically transfer some of these healing potentialitics into the psyche of the reader. The most useful critics are those who can guide us, prompt us, to get closer to the living heart of great works of imaginative literature, who can open up a circuit for the flow of energy from the imagination of the writer to that of the reader. The layers of insulation against this energy which it seems to be the main purpose of ego and education to provide, have to be stripped away.

To acquire these qualifications requires from the critic a great deal of both learning and unlearning, which will differ for each individual – unlearning much of what is taught in the academies, including the futile pursuit of a sterile objectivity. We are taught to cultivate the detached analytical intelligence. Such detachment is, in fact, the crime for which literature offers judgement and correction, the sickness for which it offers diagnosis, and, if we are receptive enough, cure. It is the source of all the other crimes which have made our survival on earth so problematical – dualism, hubris, anthropocentrism.

Of course all this, with its respect for writers, imagination, texts, is now politically incorrect. But great writers will continue to make themselves heard, and readers will continue to try to read them better, since great imaginative art is, as Hughes put it, 'the psychological component of the body's own system of immunity and self-repair', and therefore part of our essential biological survival gear.

How I didn't meet Ted Hughes

I am four years younger than Hughes, but because he did his National Service before going to Cambridge and I didn't, my first year was his third.

It was an exciting time to be in Cambridge – the wild parties, the budding poets, the lively poetry magazines, the first Hughes poems appearing in *Chequer* and *Granta* and the *St Botolph's Review* – all those activities recorded in Plath's *Journals* and in *Birthday Letters*. I must have passed Sylvia Plath a dozen times on King's Parade. But I knew nothing of those people, those parties, those publications. Cambridge English soon cured me of writing poems. But my dreams were undisturbed by smouldering foxes, as I dutifully got on with essays on Dr Johnson or whatever.

My taste in poetry at that time was for the rich and passionate. I drank deep in Donne. I was hooked on poems about animals. My favourite poems were 'The Windhover' and 'Snake'. I left Cambridge in the year of *New Lines*. Dylan Thomas, whom I had heard reading at the Cambridge Union, was dead. Eliot was writing only plays. Nothing in contemporary English poetry impinged on me until the publication of *The Hawk in the Rain* the following year. This was what I wanted.

In my first year of teaching (in adult education) *Lupercal* appeared, and Hughes's poems began to feature frequently in my classes. They could be guaranteed to generate plenty of discussion. By the time *Wodwo* appeared (1967) I was in the Extra-Mural Department at Manchester University, and had just published my first book, on Lawrence. *Wodwo* bowled me over afresh, and I was struck by the inadequacy of the critical response. So I wrote my first piece on Hughes, on the development of his work over those three books.

Our department owned at that time a residential college, Holly Royde, which was hired by BBC TV on 18 March 1969 to record a reading by Hughes. Some tickets were made available to the department, and I obtained five, so that I could take four of my students I knew to be particularly interested in Hughes. I took with me what I had written with the intention of asking Hughes to look at it and see if he felt I was on the right lines.

It was very cold and raining as I drove to Blackburn to collect the fourth of my students. From there we climbed slowly up behind a lorry onto Haslingden Moor. At the top the road straightened; I pulled out and accelerated, not realizing that at this height the rain was freezing as it hit the ground. (It was the night the Emley Moor television mast collapsed under the weight of ice.) I found I had no steering, went sideways, then backwards, crashed into a wall on one side of the road, and bounced across into the opposite wall. We ended up on our side in the ditch, the windscreen and back window gone. This was before the days of seatbelts, but because there were three passengers wedged into my back seat, no one was injured. We were eventually rescued and taken back to my house. I opened some cans of soup and a bottle of wine. We listened to all the poems Hughes had recorded, then had a hilarious party.

The next day I wrote to Hughes, sending my essay, and explaining why there had been five empty seats at his reading. I only half expected an answer. After two or three weeks I abandoned hope. Then I received a most kind and encouraging letter in which Hughes said:

> What I have actually got down on paper seems such a small part, up to now, of what I concern myself with, that it is disturbing to have my intentions divined as generously as you divine them in your paper. But it is a great change to read an article that concerns itself with the imaginative and vital interior of poetry, rather than the verbal surface exclusively, and yours seems to me both bold and sensitive in that respect, keeping the surface qualities just in the right perspective.

I did not discover until many years later why Hughes had not replied earlier. After the reading Hughes had joined up with his partner Assia and they had gone north, househunting. They found a suitable house on the North Tyne. Hughes returned to Devon and Assia to London, where she killed herself and their daughter Shura the following day. This blow had made it impossible for Hughes to continue with his great Crow project. The last of the *Crow* poems, 'A Horrible Religious Error', had been written on the train to Manchester. These circumstances made it remarkable that Hughes should have felt able to reply to me at all; but his letter encouraged me to continue to write and later to publish on him.

How I met Ted Hughes
By 1970 I had begun to collect Hughes seriously. A London bookseller friend, Ben Kane, knew Olwyn Hughes, Ted's sister

and at that time his agent. He told me that she had some of Hughes's manuscripts for sale, and made an appointment for us to visit her in Hampstead to look at them. I had still never seen Hughes, though I was familiar with his photographs. We were dumbstruck when the door was opened by Ted himself. Due to some confusion about the time of our arrival, Olwyn was out. Hughes glared suspiciously at us as though he expected us to try to sell him a set of encyclopaedias. Eventually he invited us in. Olwyn returned half an hour later, and then Ted himself went out. But the manuscripts were so many and so fascinating that we were still looking at them when he returned some two hours later. He discussed them with us affably for a while, but I had a train to catch and could not stay longer.

Though I bought some of those manuscripts, it was a year or two later when I bought the most important ones, including *Prometheus on his Crag,* that crucial work in which Hughes tried to haul himself up by his own bootstraps from the abyss of the 1960s, and tried to convert the suffering of that decade into the strength with which to make a new start. The first steps in that new life were his marriage to Carol Orchard and his decision to go into partnership with her father Jack farming at Moortown.

By 1975 we had begun to correspond regularly. I sent Hughes chapters of *The Art of Ted Hughes* as I wrote them. He replied, often at length, but his direct responses to what I had written were nearly always on matters of fact rather than interpretation. In one of his earliest letters to me (1974) Hughes wrote:

> I've tried to give your text factual support, & to suggest my debts to certain sources & sites in the way of subject matter, but everything speculative or to do with interpretation & evaluation are anybody's own business, yours as much as mine, finally. I know how absolutely meaningless it would be to try to impose mine, or attach it somehow to the poems as if it were part of them. Finally, poems belong to readers – just as houses belong to those who live in them & not to the builders.

When I showed Hughes my reading of *Prometheus on his Crag*

he said that it surprised him, 'but always into agreement'. I have certainly never felt able to take such agreement for granted.

In May I was to mount the first Hughes exhibition as part of the Ilkley Literature Festival. Ted undertook to borrow a great deal of material from Leonard Baskin, who was living near him at the time, and to leave it for me to collect from Olwyn's house, where he intended to stay on his way to the Cambridge Literature Festival. When he got to Cambridge he found it was still in the boot of his car. He stayed with Olwyn again on the return journey, but found the stuff still in his boot when he got back to Devon. We were running out of time, so I arranged to go down to Devon and collect it. He recommended that I should stay at the George in Hatherleigh, where he and Carol would join me for dinner.

I had not seen Hughes since our brief encounter in London five years earlier, so this was to be, in effect, our first proper meeting. Stories were rife about his reserve and unapproachability, particularly in relation to literary critics, several of whom had betrayed his confidences. It was a very long drive from Lancashire. I had plenty of time to think about how I would handle the meeting. I made the very wise decision not to mention his work or any literary matters until he did. We talked about our common background in West Yorkshire, about our common obsession with animals, about his farming experiences, and many other non-literary matters. We had an excellent very long-drawn-out meal and two bottles of wine. They had to throw us out at midnight. In the car park Ted opened his boot to transfer the pictures to mine, only to find he had forgotten to put them in. He invited me to lunch at his home the following day. Carol suggested that if I wanted some time to look round the area, I should go to dinner instead and stay the night.

Before dinner next day Ted took me over to see Totleigh Barton, the Devon home of the Arvon Foundation. The food (caught by Ted, cooked by Carol) was delicious. By the time I left next morning I had spent about twelve hours in Ted's company, and we were discussing his work as freely as any other topics, with no reserve at all. I remember complaining about his handwriting which I found very difficult to decipher in the manuscripts I had bought. I asked if he could read it himself. He said he could read it only during the period when he could more or less remember what he had written. This had become such a problem that he had resolved to force himself to write legibly. However, he had soon found that this produced a different kind of poetry, much more considered, deliberate, formal, a kind he didn't want to write. So he had had to revert to his hectic scribble, trying to get the words down just as they came, at least in the first drafts (drafts which he often found he could not better). I also said that I had noticed that the most revised poem in *Prometheus on his Crag*, the final poem, which existed in some fifteen drafts, had only one line which survived intact through all the revisions, but this had mysteriously disappeared from the published text – why? The line was, speaking of the vulture, 'that never harmed any living thing'. He said it was too good for the rest of the poem. The line later found its true home in *Cave Birds*.

I also remember on that first visit being shown a tiger skull, feeling the incredible weight of that upper jaw. That experience gave a new meaning to the lines in 'Tiger-Psalm': 'The tiger / Kills like the fall of a cliff'. Later, after my son Arren had proudly shown Ted his collection of rabbit and sheep bones, Ted sent him the skull of 'the first badger I ever boiled', and a fox-skull, and a rattlesnake's rattle 'to scare your mum'.

On subsequent visits to Devon, I was taken to Moortown farm to see his great red Devon bull, and for walks along some of the salmon rivers near his home. It was sad how often he was showing me places where hosts of salmon or sea trout 'used to be' when he first fished those rivers.

Gaudete and *Cave Birds*

In April 1977 Hughes sent me an advance copy of the first major product of his new life, *Gaudete*. In it he wrote 'The head is older than the book'. Of course the modern head, almost severed from its inheritance, needs just such a book as *Gaudete* to reactivate its connections with the whole man, thereby releasing imagination. *Gaudete* fertilized my own imagination more than any other book I have read. I had been writing poems again for a decade, but at the rate of perhaps one a year. As soon as I began *Gaudete*, they started to come at the rate of more like one a week, and were much better than anything I had written before, though some of them were so strange that I could offer only tentative interpretations. They came quite unbidden, and were not at all attempts to imitate anything in *Gaudete*. I sent them to Hughes, who liked them (though he was almost unfailingly positive about other people's verse, on the principle that the bad man calls the misses, the good man the hits). For the first time I had managed to make use of a dream, in a poem called 'The Nightingale Man'.

Of this poem Hughes wrote to me: 'The dream is also effective – completely mysterious, unfaked, and disturbing'.

On one visit to my house, Ted spent an hour gazing intently and silently at a single fish, a flame blenny, in my marine tropical aquarium. He had used this method in writing some of his own poems (such as 'Eclipse'). I subsequently did the same thing, gazing hour after hour at a cleaner wrasse or a mantis shrimp, and produced some good, for me, poems. Hughes spoke of the 'microscopically-exact fish in their intent lives' in the beautiful and generous little essay on simplicity in poetry he wrote as an introduction to my only published collection of poems, *The Reef*.

I wanted to share my excitement about *Gaudete* and explore it more deeply. I invited all the friends and students I could think of who were interested in Hughes to come to my house one evening a week to discuss it. No fee, no obligation to attend every week, free snacks and drinks. For the whole summer there was an average of about six of us every week. We went through the text page by page, and at the end of each meeting I allocated each student a passage to prepare for the following week. We got so hooked on these meetings – some of the most fruitful teaching I have ever done (if you can call such a common pursuit teaching) – that when we came to the end of *Gaudete* we immediately embarked on *Cave Birds*. Out of these meetings came my chapters on these works in

the second (1978) edition of *The Art of Ted Hughes*. When I sent
the chapter on *Gaudete* to Hughes he replied:

> You read *Gaudete* as I hoped it might be read. If nothing of that
> is taken into account, the thing can only seem confused and
> arbitrary. Once that's taken into account the lines can be seen in
> focus, and judged properly. It's like a mathematical problem –
> to which the style is the correct answer. It's only when the whole
> problem's understood, that the style will be seen for what it is.
> To hear it called crude, clumsy etc. (all of which it is) means that
> the reader hasn't understood why I took so much trouble to
> make it that way.

To be told by the writer on whom one has written (or the ghost of
a dead writer): 'You read this work as I hoped it would be read'
seems to me the ultimate justification for a critic. This is very
different from saying that a critic's reading should coincide with
that of the author. It is characteristic of imagination that it brings
up truths from a far deeper level than that on which the writer's
own conscious intention or understanding operates. These
meanings may be profoundly disturbing to the writer, who may
resist or repudiate them. A writer's interpretation of his own
work may be a smokescreen. As Lawrence said: 'Never trust the
artist, trust the tale'.

By this time Hughes was regularly sending me his work in
progress. I believe I was on at least one occasion able to make a
significant contribution, when I persuaded him to restore five
poems he had decided to drop from *Cave Birds*. They were 'After
the first fright', 'She seemed so considerate', 'Something was
happening', 'Only a little sleep, a little slumber' and 'A green
mother'.

Hughes wrote to me:

> I'd like to thank you for your remarks about *Cave Birds*,
> because they made me dig out those pieces I'd deleted, and so it
> comes about that I rediscover their rough virtues, so much
> better than what I tried to replace them with, as you so rightly

complain, and I think probably better than the main sequence, certainly better than many of them. In fact now I look at them I realize they were the beginning of an attempt to open myself in a different direction, a very necessary direction for me, the only real direction, and I'm aghast at the time and density of folly that has passed since I lost sight of it.

Hughes's letters

For such a prolific writer, and someone who spent so much time of his time outdoors, it is amazing that Hughes found time to write so many letters (many of them very long) to so many people, including a high proportion of strangers and children. Many of his letters have been quoted in books and articles, but almost all of these are about his own work. When Hughes's letters are published, this will be by no means the only area of interest. I was particularly delighted, in his letters to me, by the little Lawrencean vignettes of the spirit of place. Two examples; first his response to Australia in 1976.

My 5 days, or 6, in that country was one of the best jaunts I've ever had. I saw very little of the land. Just the primaeval scrub of Ti trees between the bijou bungalows on the promontory south of Melbourne. Then on my last day I visited a farm – an 18c manor farm – 70 miles or so outside Adelaide. I got a taste of it there. The whole place hit me very hard & deep. The most peculiar thing is the light – a glare even when there's cloud. It casts a weird disastrous starkness over everything – like a primitive painting. A dream brilliance & strangeness. Everything stands or moves in some eerie significance – rather sinister & very beautiful. I couldn't get over it. And I couldn't quite locate exactly what created the impression – except the light. Every bird behaves at least as queerly as our cuckoos. And they have a class of cries utterly different & unique – imagine the calls of lizards & prehistoric freaks. Cries completely unmodified by the revisions & bird-masterpieces of the last 50 million years. And behaviour to go with the cries.

[239]

The second passage from 1980 describes Hughes's trip to Alaska with his son Nicholas.

Alaska was everything I'd hoped. Everything happened I wanted to happen, & a whole lot more. We caught salmon until we were actually sick of catching them. We got ourselves off great lakes (living time, 5 minutes of immersion – so cold) by the skin of our teeth two or 3 times. We fished alongside bears. Lay awake listening to wolves. And generally sleep-walked through that dreamland. Unearthly valleys of flowers between snow mountains. Miles of purple lupins. 300 thousand people in a country the size of all Europe. Mostly new residents – fleeing from the States for one of several usual reasons – a picked lot of dreamers, escapists, self-elected red indians, hoodlums & generally infatuated freedom addicts – it is extraordinarily free. But the Americans are there like migrants resting in transit – a very shallow hold. And the Indians & Eskimos are gradually getting all their claims back – interesting.

Weird
My work on Hughes has involved me in several very strange experiences.

In 1971 I felt like trying my hand at a Crow poem. Not in a spirit of parody or pastiche, but as a tribute to the all-purpose usefulness of Crow as a poetic catalyst. I called it 'Crow Goes to the Movies'. A couple of years later I learned that Liverpool University Library had a Hughes collection. I sent for a catalogue. Among the unpublished manuscripts I found to my horror one called 'Crow Goes to the Movies'. I had circulated several copies of my poem. Someone, I assumed, had passed one of these off as a genuine Hughes poem. I went over to Liverpool to look at the collection. 'Crow Goes to the Movies' *was* a genuine Hughes poem, bearing no resemblance to mine. But what are the odds against both of us choosing that oddly Americanized title?

In 1978 I went with an American friend Gerald Lacy following the Lawrence trail in northern Italy and Switzerland. Somehow we got into the habit of telling each other our dreams immediately on waking. In the past I had very rarely been able to remember dreams, but this immediate telling fixed them in the memory. During our stay in Tarquinia we had an idyllic day visiting the Etruscan necropolis at Cerveteri. That night I had a very strange dream which did not at the time seem to have any connection with the visit. A week later, in Switzerland, Gerald suggested that we should go our separate ways for a day, that each of us should write a short story, and that we should read them to each other after dinner. I set off towards a beautiful Alpine meadow which I had seen the previous day. By the time I got there, the story was written in my head, for a connection had suddenly occurred to me between the Etruscan tombs and my dream. The story is extremely short, so I can give it in full.

It was late May and a late spring. The sun was bright but not burning. There were flowers everywhere. The air was rich with scents, and the cypresses rustled softly to themselves. We were among the first to arrive that morning. A group of screaming schoolchildren was soon left behind: and we soon lost each other in the maze of tombs.

The area of the necropolis would have looked tiny on any map; but because of the crowdedness of the tombs and their apparently random arrangement, in reality it seemed vast. It had nothing whatever of the gloom, the clammy morbidity of an English graveyard. Here the word resurrection seemed more than the empty token it has become in Christianity. Somewhere, in some form, the Etruscans who had been buried here are dancing again and smiling still, in this world or another.

I strayed further and further from the trodden paths, glimpsing my friend in the distance less and less frequently. Birdsongs were now the only sounds. Most of the tombs were circular, about fifty feet in diameter, and domed. The tumuli were all wildly overgrown, and ablaze with broom. Handsome green lizards sunned themselves on the walls, posed to be photographed, then, at the crucial moment, scuttled off towards the dark entrances, and stood for a moment at the thresholds, brighteyed against the blackness. Steps led down to the entrances, most of which were blocked with rubble. Some of the tombs were flooded, and the stairs disappeared into a phosphorescent green scum. A few were open, and cobwebs guarded their darkness and silence.

Time slowed as the sun climbed. I walked through waist-high flowers round the circumference of a high tomb, and suddenly came upon an opening at my feet the size of a house, a sunken court. An intact staircase led down to it from a far corner. I had seen nothing like it before. I could see no way to the stair but by leaping a five-foot gap with an unsure footing and a fall of some twenty feet. I jumped it safely and descended the stair. There was a doorway in the middle of each wall. All were blocked. But one not completely. I crawled through. When my eyes adjusted to the darkness I could see nothing but rubble-strewn empty chambers, and was about to turn back when I caught a glimmer of light ahead – another exit. With great difficulty I scrambled through.

With every step the temperature fell and the air became more dank. I became aware of a greenish eerie light. I emerged at the head of a steep valley with strange primitive trees and giant mosses and ferns. The sides of the valley were close and sheer and the sky looked far up. It was cold, and there were neither birds nor flowers. Nothing moved in the unnatural stillness. I moved slowly forward, intruding on the last fastness of an earlier world-age, long before the Etruscans, long before civilizations existed or joy was known.

Beneath the ancient trees like standing fossils, something took shape, something brown and beastlike. It did not move. I approached in fear. It was some great Elk-like beast with massive antlers. But what was wrong with it? Its stillness was not the stillness of a cocked lizard, nor yet the stillness of death. With a pang of horror I saw that it had no eyes, just black holes where its eyes had been. It must be dead, long dead. But it was not dead. It made a sound, a sound I heard with my spine, the sound of aeons of accumulated agony and resignation. The beast could neither live nor die. It stood in an attitude of utter wretchedness. And I saw that what I had taken to be antlers were not all antlers. Among the antlers were shafts of wood driven into the skull and wedged there. The beast had long ago lost the will or the strength to try to dislodge them. Fear gave way to compassion. Very gently I touched one of the smaller shafts. The beast did not move. I grasped the shaft and gently pulled. Slowly it came away, leaving a bottomless hole like the eye-sockets. Slowly I pulled out another and another, inching them out as gently as I could, though the beast made neither sound nor movement. An hour or so it took to remove all the shafts. I stood back and wondered what the point of my intervention was. The beast had stood thus for centuries. Surely it could feel nothing. Then I remembered that sound. Had the beast actually made it, or had I imagined it?

Now I looked at the cavernous face of the beast, and the beast looked at me. With its empty eye-sockets I knew that it looked at me. And I knew that, though I saw no tears, it wept. And I knew that its weeping was a remission of its agony.

On my way home through London I saw a billboard advertising a magazine called *Bananas*, which announced that the current number contained a new short story by Ted Hughes. I bought a copy. The story was called 'The Head'. It was a long story, but the further I read, the more aware I became that it was the same story as 'The Beast', not only in essentials, but occasionally in detail and even phraseology. In each story a modern man, from our despiritualized world, makes a journey into a nightmare world, which is also the animal world and the spirit world. In each case he must pass through the territory of a primitive race with an animistic religion. In each case the dreamworld is a dark, steep, heavily forested valley. In 'The Beast' the ancient trees are 'like standing fossils'; in 'The Head' the forest is 'like a cave full of stalagmites'. In each story the sacredness of the animal/spirit world is violated by senseless, barbaric cruelty. Each narrator is watched by an elk. Mine has 'massive antlers', Hughes's has 'antlers the breadth of a lounge'. My elk looks at me 'with its empty eye-sockets'; his looks at him 'with his dead brilliant eye'. In each story what should kill an animal, many stakes driven into its head, or many bullets fired into its body, fails to do so. It refuses to die. In each story the narrator is transformed, purified, by 'animal wounds and animal pain'. There is much more in Hughes's story, but it contains the whole of mine. Hughes's story must have been written first. How was it transmitted across Europe to me in my sleep in Tarquinia?

I sent the story to Hughes, expecting him to comment on the astonishing similarities. Instead he sent me the following analysis of it:

Your dream-story was very impressive. Quite convincing. Interestingly & well written, and unforgettable. How do you interpret it? The beast is, I imagine, among other things, your original being in all its undeveloped aspects. The great stakes in its head were probably – among other things – all the theories & ideas, derived from your reading etc, about this original self, which are not natural to it – i.e. have not developed naturally out of it, but have been imposed on it by you, in your thinking about yourself. These were a torture to it, a fake head-load, a false crown. The fact that you took these out – that you were able to find the beast & take those terrible stakes out means – among the other things – that you have inwardly come to an understanding of the artificiality & wrongness of those notions, & have inwardly – by some inward change – removed them. Rejected & rubbished them. The beast weeps, because you have released him from these misunderstandings, which were like monstrous electrodes of imposed signals, having nothing to do with his real truth & because you have, by implication, recognized his real nature, and are concerned for it. The next dream in the series he will not be blind, & probably won't even be a beast. Interpreted like this, it records a big change in your life – the transition from an intellectualized steerage (and mismanagement) of your real power, which actually immobilized it – 'froze up' your life in some way, to a phase in which, we hope, it will reveal its true direction & possibilities, under your understanding respect.

Propitious dream. Though it depends how you follow it up in your behaviour. No doubt there are other interpretations. But I think it's important to interpret dreams – if at all possible – positively. And this is so general, it seems quite clearly good.

All this was new to me; but it may well be true for all I know.

There was a sequel to this story. In 1986 I bought Aidan Dunne's monograph on the Irish painter Barrie Cooke, because it contained Hughes's poem 'The Great Irish Pike', illustrated by Cooke. Here I found a magnificent painting by Cooke called *Megacarous Hibernicus* (1983). It is a painting of my beast, its face a mask of blood. Dunne writes of it:

> *Megacarous Hibernicus* is a cloudy, epic vision of an elk, its body in profile, its head, and the great spread of its antlers angled towards us. Hazy, emergent, it stands against and blends into a moist, dark blanket of space, like a murky soup of time, suffused with a misty light. . . . It is a ghostly presence, hazy and evanescent, but the pale shafts of skeletal bone, the red sinewy trails of pigment, flowering antlers webbed with veins, and its heroic, questing attitude, surveying us through the centuries, indicates a resurrected, sentient state.

I like to think that Cooke's purer vision represents a later stage of the resurrection of the same elk, the same violated but unkillable holy life in our common consciousness.

I later discovered that Cooke and Hughes used to go round old Irish houses and museums together looking for skeletons of elks.

A couple of years later came another strange incident. I was working on my bibliography of Hughes in the Manchester reference library. I had been working all day, and was tired and hungry, but I intended to stay until the library closed at nine, then treat myself to a Chinese meal. I was going through bound volumes of *The Spectator* looking for contributions by Hughes. Fortunately, they were indexed. I had the volumes on a trolley. As I had checked them, I took them from the top shelf and put them on the bottom. I picked up a new volume and looked in the index. 'Hughes, Ted, 859'. I turned to page 859 only to find that it consisted entirely of adverts. Assuming that in my tiredness I had misread the page number, I turned back to the index, only to find that there was no entry under Ted Hughes at all. Where had I got that page 859? I put that volume on the bottom shelf and picked up the next. The index read 'Hughes, Ted, 859'. And on that page was his poem 'Poltergeist'.

The Silence of Cordelia
Of all the many books of criticism I have read, Hughes's *Shakespeare and the Goddess of Complete Being* fulfils my criteria for criticism far more than any other. It takes us close to the living heart not just of a great work, but of the entire corpus of the greatest of all writers. And the amazing thing is that it is almost all so new and surprising. How can so many of us have wrestled with Shakespeare for so long and made so little progress towards his essential meanings? John Moat felt that Shakespeare had had to wait 500 years 'to get a thorough hearing'. Hughes steeped himself all his adult life in Shakespeare. Marina Warner wondered whether there could be anyone else alive who knew Shakespeare so well.

The whole book stems from the hypothesis that 'every poet does no more than find metaphors for his own nature'. The exploration of what metaphors Shakespeare found took Hughes over twenty years, several drafts, and, in its final form, over 500 pages.

In 1971 Hughes had published a highly pregnant essay, 'Shakespeare's Poem'. This essay was clearly the embryonic form of a full-scale study of Shakespeare's complete works.

However, it seemed unlikely that it would ever emerge in that form, since Hughes's criticism at that time had been entirely in the form of brief essays, introductions and reviews.

One reader, Donya Feuer of the Royal Dramatic Theatre in Stockholm, was fascinated by the theatrical possibilities inherent in Hughes's essay, the possibility, for example, of combining extracts from the last fifteen plays 'hugely shuffled and rearranged to make a *perpetuum mobile* maze of metamorphic episodes, play dissolving into play, characters going through their transformations, in and out of each other's worlds, like supernatural, dying and resurrected entities in a real myth' [*Shakespeare and the Goddess of Complete Being*, xii]. Hughes had independently been thinking of expanding his ideas on Shakespeare, and decided to do so in the form of a series of letters to Donya Feuer under the title of *The Silence of Cordelia*. Hughes sent these letters to me in batches as he wrote them, inviting my comments. We exchanged many long letters about the book over the next several months. Just what effect they had is hard to say.

In the final published book, Hughes makes many attempts to summarize his approach. The best of these I can find is tucked away on pages 392–3:

Confronting the Goddess of Divine Love, the Goddess of Complete Being, the ego's extreme alternatives are either to reject her and attempt to live an independent, rational, secular life or to abnegate the ego and embrace her love with "total, unconditional love", which means to become a saint, a holy idiot, possessed by the Divine Love. The inevitability of the tragic idea which Shakespeare projects with such "divine" completeness is that there is no escape from one choice or the other. Man will always choose the former, simply because once he is free of a natural, creaturely awareness of the divine indulgence which permits him to exist at all, he wants to live his own life, and he has never invented a society of saints that was tolerable. In other worlds, always, one way or another, he rejects the Goddess. This is the first phase of the tragedy. Then follows his correction: his "madness" against the Goddess, the Puritan crime which leads directly to his own tragic self-destruction, from which he can escape only after the destruction of his ego – being reborn through the Flower rebirth, becoming a holy idiot, renouncing his secular independence, and surrendering once again to the Goddess.

From the human point of view, obviously the whole business is monstrous: tragic on a cosmic scale, where the only easements are in the possibilities of a temporary blessing from the Goddess (an erotic fracture in the carapace of the tragic hero) or of becoming a saint. There is a third possibility, in some degree of self-anaesthesia, some kind of living death.

But man has no more choice in the basic arrangement than the blue-green algae.

Hughes calls this his 'tragic equation', though it is far from being some mechanical formula he has invented; it is no less than a complex, all-embracing myth, which Shakespeare forged out of his inheritance of classical mythology and Gnostic and Alchemical wisdom, all transformed in the crucible of his life and times, as his supreme attempt to convert apparently random and painful experience into a process of self-transformation:

The secret of Shakespeare's unique development lies in this ability (in most departments of life it would be regarded as a debility) to embrace the inchoate, as-if-supernatural actuality, and be overwhelmed by it, be dismantled and even shattered by it, without closing his eyes, and then to glue himself back together, with a new, greater understanding of the abyss, all within the confines of a drama, and to do this once every seven months, year after year for twenty-four years. The point here is that though every play is made up, to some degree, of an amalgam of his earlier styles, each one opens a core of poetry, in the death-rebirth episode, that is absolutely new. In other words, the episode of death-rebirth that the Equation formulates, and that each play of the sequence dramatizes, is the systole-diastole of Shakespeare's poetic life, the fundamental rhythmic event of his perpetual inspiration and his perpetual, convulsive growth. This is another way of saying that the shamanic dream, in which the Goddess, as a boar, over-whelmed his intellectual ego, must have been an in-built, recurrent event in his psychic life. [479]

And it is not only a matter of self-transformation. Shakespeare simultaneously expresses what Hughes calls 'the fundamental human challenge'. The equation is equally applicable, that is, not only to Shakespeare, but to the template of many of the classics of Western literature (including *The Oresteia*, the Theban plays of Sophocles, *The Bacchae, Sir Gawain and the Green Knight*, 'The Ancient Mariner', *Moby Dick, The Scarlet Letter*, Hopkins, Eliot, Golding and Hughes himself, especially *Crow, Cave Birds* and *Gaudete*), and to the present world predicament, the ecological crisis.

I had little difficulty with the equation itself, being already familiar with most of it as adumbrated in the 1971 essay. My problems arose with Hughes's detailed application of the equation to individual works. My responses were of three kinds: complete approval and enlightenment; initial shock or reserva-tions gradually broken down by Hughes's argument; or outrage, at what seemed to me the use of the equation as a Procrustean bed. Naturally most of our correspondence focused on the third category. The readings which troubled me most were of *Measure for Measure, Hamlet* and *The Tempest*. It cannot be coincidence that these are the three plays with which I am most familiar, on which I have written at greatest length myself. Therefore I had invested a great deal in my own readings of these plays.

Hughes insists again and again that his application of the equation to the last fifteen plays (and some earlier ones) is not intended to be exclusive. In some cases it might be possible to account for almost the whole play in terms of the equation, certainly the heart of it; in others the equation is a ghostly presence behind a play concerned primarily with other matters (as in a Magic Eye picture, a bold three-dimensional image stands just behind a complex, apparently unrelated pattern, if one can only bring it into focus). Nevertheless, I could not reconcile my reading of Isabella with his, and our long argument about her ended in stalemate. Or rather did not end at all, since we were still trying to convince each other only a fortnight before his death.

In the first draft it was Hughes's intention to make *King Lear* the culmination of the book's argument. Hence all the plays after *King Lear* received very cursory treatment. Five of the letters were devoted to *King Lear*, only three, two of them very short, to *The Tempest*. So my problem with Hughes's account of *The Tempest* was that he seemed not to develop its importance as the final conclusive round in the battle between the rational, puritanical human male and the Goddess. I wrote to him (31 August 1990):

> The book seems to end very abruptly. Nor do I come away from your reading of *The Tempest* with any very clear idea of how your application of the equation affects your overall interpretation of the play. Unlike any of your other readings, you seem to be applying the equation to each character separately, without ever pulling the whole thing together. The nearest thing to a conclusion seems to come too early (p.5) . . . I think you need – either at the very end or between your itemizing of the plot and your coda on the language – another page or two to sum up the meaning of the play as a whole and what it tells us of Shakespeare's final position in relation to the Goddess. How does the play constitute 'the completion of Shakespeare's spiritual task'? Is Prospero no more than Adonis who, having narrowly escaped the boar, goes into hiding or retreat for decades to perfect his defences against Venus until he is powerful enough to exclude her from his magic circle? Does he succeed in this? Does Shakespeare approve of the attempt? Or are you saying that the attempt is doomed because, though Sycorax may be dead and Venus distant, the boar survives in Antonio and Caliban even on the island, and presumably

marauds everywhere in the world beyond, where Prospero will be without his book and staff?

I enclose a copy of a talk I gave last year on *The Tempest* to a group of A-level students. It had to be both simplified and comprehensive, so much of it is irrelevant to your purposes, but you might find one or two interesting points in it.

To this Hughes replied:

I'm rewriting Section 5. Everything you say about it I also feel. The introduction to that section is already the largest in the book (25 written pages), & begins to say what I mean. Your *Tempest* lecture is full of points. Basically, I feel I'm on your wavelength throughout – & I think it gives me the dog to round up my own scattered flock.

Section 5, which became Chapter 6 in the published book, grew to 120 pages, and became the book's new culmination, with its wonderful material on the masque and on the relevance of Dido to *The Tempest*.

Thrilling as it was to receive this material in so new-minted, almost molten a form, the speed of its production was awesome. The first letter was dated 23 April 1990, the last 14 June 1990. They occupy over 230 pages of typescript, an average of four-and-a-half pages a day. And at the same time that Hughes was writing the later letters, he was rewriting and expanding the earlier ones, and doing a phenomenal amount of reading. And *The Silence of Cordelia* was not the only project he was working on at the time.

Hughes himself came to see that whole period of his life as an evasion of what wanted to get itself expressed in his poetry, the material which surfaced, too late, as *Birthday Letters*. In June 1998 he wrote to me:

The arrest of what I might have made of Crow, and of that material in other truly creative works, held me till I more or less abandoned the effort – and from the piece about Baskin (took a year almost), the piece about Eliot (a few months) the new Introduction to Ecco Press republication of the Selected Shakes, which turned into Shakespeare and the Goddess (2 years, staying up till 3 & 4 a.m. – destroying my immune system), I took refuge in prose. Oh, yes, & the Coleridge essay & revisions of the Winter Pollen pieces, maybe the best part of a year, though it was all done by early 1994. Still – 5 or 6 years of nothing but prose – nothing but burning the foxes. (That fox was telling – prose is destroying you physically, literally: maybe not others, but you, yes.)

The fox to which he referred was the smouldering fox which visited him in a dream in Cambridge, saying: 'You are killing us' – killing, that is, the demons of his innermost, most authentic, most natural self.

That body of prose constitutes some of the most valuable criticism ever produced, but produced, it seems, at the cost not only of unimaginable poetic achievements, such as *The Life and Songs of the Crow* might have been, but of many more years of life.

Manuscripts

In 1994 Hughes told me that he was thinking of selling his own collection of his manuscripts, but that before doing so, he needed to go through them to pick out what he wanted, for various reasons, to keep – unfinished work to which he might wish to return, for example. He was daunted by the extent of the task, and asked me if I could help. I went down to Devon to have a look at the material, and found over fifty large cardboard boxes brimming with manuscripts.

I set to work at once, making a descriptive list, beginning with the *Crow* archive. This consisted of nearly 1,000 pages. Most of the material was unpublished, a great deal of it in prose, describing stations of Crow's quest beyond the end of *Crow*. It was frustrating to know just how much of the great abandoned 'epic folk tale' *The Life and Songs of the Crow* already existed. When I asked Hughes if he would ever finish it, he replied that it was not something that he could return to for a few hours at a time, alongside other commitments. Crow would have to be allowed to take him over again, draw him back into his world for months on end. Perhaps he could never again recapture the complex state of mind and feeling out of which Crow had come into being.

The manuscripts of *A Primer of Birds* was also fascinating in that it illustrated a method of composition I had not come across before, though Hughes said he often used it. In the middle of a page he drew a circle inside which he jotted down all the ideas he had thought of using in the poem, clustering around the bird itself at the centre – all the attributes and associations and images of that bird he could think of. His development of these might spread outwards into larger circles. Or the developing ideas might be connected by lines to areas outside the circle, which might become new circles, round which still further satellite circles might orbit. When the page was full, looking like either a mandala or a diagram of molecular structure, it was time to move on to the first draft proper, incorporating perhaps half of the material generated.

A major problem, of course, was how to resist reading every word of the manuscripts. Another was the illegibility of much of what I needed to read. I was still working full-time, and could therefore not spare many hours a week. By the time I had finished my reports on *Crow, A Primer of Birds,* and *River* I had taken several months, and would clearly never get through the fifty boxes. Ann Skea volunteered to help, and made a start. But at this point Ted realized that the information we were able to extract, as little more than a list, did not give him enough to enable him to make the decisions he had to make. No one but himself could do the job adequately.

From my own point of view, my months of work had been by no means wasted. Working with these manuscripts not only gave me access to a great deal of fascinating unpublished material, but also demonstrated afresh what I already knew from the manuscripts I had bought, that almost every Hughes poem is the end product of a long labour, not a labour of polishing and perfecting, but of going back to the beginning and starting afresh along a slightly different tack, or of abandoning sections and letting new ones grow. In poetry as in gardening it seems that 'growth follows the knife'.

In 1997 the bulk of the collection was sold to Emory University.

Postscript

Our family holiday in the summer of 1998 was in Cornwall. Our route involved passing quite close to North Tawton. I knew that Hughes had been unwell, but knew nothing of his terminal illness. I wrote asking if it would be convenient to call, as we had done on several earlier visits to the West Country. Ted's invitation, alas, arrived the day after we had departed, so we didn't call. His later description of the meeting we might have had was typically in terms of giving – 'You could have had cream tea and I could have given you some Laureate sherry, and shown Arren my skulls, and given him a skin or two'. That particular joy is now lost for ever, but there were many other times we did not miss, and can never lose.

Perhaps what those of us privileged to know Ted will most remember him for is his generosity. But that same generosity of spirit informed all his writing, and remains available to everyone. At the time of his death I was reminded of the words of Frieda Lawrence on the death of her husband D. H. Lawrence, in the year Hughes was born:

What he had seen and felt and known he gave in his writing to his fellow men, the splendour of living, the hope of more and more life he had given them, a heroic and immeasurable gift.

PENELOPE SHUTTLE

Talisman

In the late 1960s I published a novella, my first work of fiction. Soon afterwards I received a letter from Ted about my book, full of encouragement and open understanding. It was a lovely letter which still acts for me as a door thrown open into language, as a welcome and a permission to be a writer myself.

Poetry is contagious. We catch poetry from one another. About four years ago, I found myself going through a dry spell. I cast about for a strong experience in poetry to bring me back to my own sources and energies. I found such a book. To be accurate, it is *Three Books*, the edition comprising *Remains of Elmet*, *Cave Birds* and *River*. As I re-read Ted's poems I was immersed in the flowing manifold world of the imagination. Via these poems, the exhilaration of their diction, their grace and power, I found my way through to my own imaginative world again. They acted as a wonderful vaccine of inspiration. I relished versing again.

In Ted's poetry we find images of such a charge of meaning they become an inseparable part of ourself, of an inner psychic theatre. Often when I am thinking of nothing in particular (a creative enough state in itself), or walking, or doing yoga, or feeling unhappy, or whatever, images from Ted's poems surface in my mind with a mingle of familiarity and yet of huge surprise. These are poem-talismans, the poetic equivalent of a lucky charm or soul stone slipped into your mental pocket, a magical and protecting permanent connection with reality.

One of these talismans (from the inexhaustible supply available from Hughes's work) is the poem 'An Eel' from *River*. The particular phrase 'the nun of water' haunts me. It is a productive haunting, with all the shiveriness of the unforeseen real. The eel is established in complete eelhood. She courses through us, bringing us into accord with that in our own nature which contains or answers eelhood, eel-ness. The poem concludes:

> Her life is a cell
> Sealed from event, her patience
> Global and furthered with love
> By the bending stars as if she
> Were earth's sole initiate. Alone
> In her millions, the moon's pilgrim,
> The nun of water.

The poem is full of wonder, intimate endurance and active tranquillity. She, the eel, is us. We are her.

Another talisman: the two gold bears, the 'creatures of light' from 'That Morning' (from *River*). Henry Beston has said of animals that 'in a world older and more complete than ours they move finished and complete, gifted with extensions of the senses we have lost or never attained.' The poem acknowledges this, and then goes on to make a shared bridge between the bears and the watching man; sharing a world, sharing senses, sharing the light of the world. We see and feel the human in the bear, the animal in the human.

An imaginal space is created, and the world poured into it, for us. The golden innocence of the bears eating 'the pierced salmon' is illumination for and of us.

The poem makes it available to us, like the light, like an air that oxygenates the imagination. The bears recur to me again and again, when my waiting mind and spirit need their aid.

Any poet's task nowadays is to stand firm against the pollution of language by tabloidization, by lives valued only as gossip, by consumer-speak, by the word-webs of propaganda being spun all around us: this pollution causes unreality.

In Ted's work we find him writing as an ecologist in both senses: speaking on behalf of the burdened and desecrate world of nature, and also as ecologist of language and of the imagination.

My third talisman-poem is 'A Green Mother' (from *Cave Birds*). This poem, with its tender delicate precise and heartbreaking revelations of death experienced as a return to the earth, as continuity with the very core of our planet, releases us from our fears. It says that the afterlife is the earth, is our mother, nature. There is meaning in our lives and our deaths. The poem promises us this. It is a safeguard against despair, and a mirror of profoundest reality.

> This earth is the sweetness
> Of all the heavens. It is Heaven's mother.
> The grave is her breast, her nipple in its dark aura.
> Her milk is unending life.
>
> You shall see
> How tenderly she wipes her child's face clean
>
> Of the bitumen of blood and the smoke of tears.

30 October 1998

Yesterday evening we heard of Ted's death on the radio news. It seemed incredible, impossible. A disbelief of grief shook us. The words written above to celebrate Ted's seventieth birthday have now become part of our farewells.

I remember we stayed with Carol and Ted in Devon one particular summer in the early 70s. At this time Ted was farming. They had a bull. One afternoon we watched Ted gently wrestle a new ring into the nose of a red and white bull. He put his arms in a powerful embrace around the bull's neck. The combination of strength and concern in his armlock struggle with the bemused and irritable bull are an abiding image for me of Ted, mirroring his power over and love for language.

I am very sad that I will never see Ted again. Meeting him was always an occasion, an event. Unselfconsciously, from the depths of his nature, he lived each moment as a poet. Nothing of him was kept in different compartments; you received his whole unswerving unity of self, that woke you up to life, both its rough and its smooth.

He has been champion and exemplar of the possibilities of poetry in our lives and it is of him we can say: 'The world, like Dionysus, is torn to pieces by pure intellect; but the poet is Zeus; he has swallowed the heart of the world, and he can reproduce it as a living body.' *

* Owen Barfield: *Poetic Diction*, quoted in *The World of Poetry*, Clive Sansom.

ALAN SILLITOE

Ted Hughes: A Short Memoir

The coffin in which Ted lay, on the floor below the pulpit in North Tawton church, seemed huge, far too big and heavy ever to be carried away on human shoulders, but the pallbearers did their job and lifted it, slow marched up the aisle to the music of Elgar's *Nimrod* – fitting music for a hunter before the Lord. This was the only part of the service at which I felt that tears might come, because now it was more than obvious that he couldn't be anything but dead, the body at least out of everyone's life forever.

It was always my notion that Ted would have been writing some kind of obituary for me, but these days God seems to have got his hands on a machine gun, and is no respecter of a few odd years between contemporaries. Why he should have gone first I'll never know.

When I received the Hawthornden Prize for *The Loneliness of the Long Distance Runner* it was the custom that the winner would be present at the ceremony of whoever was awarded it the following year. This happened to be Ted Hughes for *The Hawk in the Rain*, and we met on the steps of a house in St James's Square, in the summer of 1961, which makes him one of my oldest friends.

Sylvia Plath was there, as was Ruth Fainlight (our wives), both poets and American. Hughes and myself were (though it's stretching a point for me) from 'the North', and in the following weeks we ate dinner in each other's flats. Ruth and I must have been among the first to call on them when they bought Court Green a couple of months later.

Hughes was diffident and modest, even taciturn, but what enlivened our gatherings was a sense of humour, laughter almost taking up as much time as speech, as if we were plugged into the same rich vein. In 1962 Ruth and I went to Tangier for the year with our baby son David, and at the end of that time, after Ted and Sylvia had split up, Ruth arranged to stay with her for a month while I was in Russia. Tragically, Sylvia killed herself, and we often wonder whether she would have done so had we been in England. Suicides deserve pity, but they have much to answer for.

Our friendship with Ted lasted. One night at Court Green, sometime in the 1970s, we sat at table with his sister Olwyn, deploring the fact that poetry wasn't cheaper and more widely available. Wondering what to do about it, we spent the time over several bottles and a long dinner working out details of The Giveaway Press. Poems would be printed on the cheapest of paper and sold on street corners for only a penny or two. The result, after a couple of years (and we later laughed about it), was The Rainbow Press, each plush and boxed volume costing about seventy-five pounds!

On another convivial evening Ted and I worked out the logistics of a trip to the beaches of Gallipoli. His father had been an infantryman there in 1915, and had told Ted that the winnings of a pontoon school among the troops, amounting to several hundred sovereigns, had been buried in the sand and must still be there. We opened maps and reckoned up distances, calculated the number of days to drive there, and the supplies to take. That did not materialize either, all of us having more important things to do.

Hughes retreated more and more into himself as the years went by, which was understandable, but to me he wasn't the silent ox-like and morose creature many people imagine. The closeness and rapport remained, in that he always sent copies of his books to me, and I reciprocated with copies of mine, both offering comments in our letters. In later years we could be relied on to leave each other alone because, as Hughes wrote in a letter: 'As you get older, guarding your time has to be the greatest aim,' as indeed it always had been and still is with me.

On 1 January 1997 he called at our place in Somerset on his way to London with Roy Davids. In those two or three hours the mood was as open and free as at any time before. Why he was going to London we didn't know, though it may have had something to do with his illness, about which I had only heard rumours.

Whatever it was, he wouldn't tell, being reticent about such things, but I didn't imagine, as we waved him off, that it was the last time I'd see him.

PETER STOTHARD

Election '97 and Ted Hughes's
Final Reading

On 14 April 1997, *The Times* was in the thick of a general election campaign and its editor Peter Stothard was negotiating to bring together the two main party leaders for the first time in British electoral history, for a televised prime ministerial debate. The behind-the-scenes battle over this battle was the consuming topic at the newspaper when 1,000 *Times* readers, with the Editor in the chair, gathered at the Institute of Education in Bloomsbury to hear a poetry recital by Ted Hughes and Seamus Heaney from their anthology *The School Bag*. This was the last public reading that Ted Hughes ever gave. What follows is part of Peter Stothard's election notebook for that night. A shortened version of it appeared in *The Times* on the day after Hughes's death.

When Ted Hughes said the word 'Sex' the full front rows of men and women, mainly women, swayed as though a wind had blown through grass. Hughes was reading from Walt Whitman, from *Song of Myself:* 'out of the dimness opposite equals advance, always substance and increase, always sex . . .'

When he reached the word 'sex' it was as though he had touched everyone with a breath. The movement was a wave. It was only small. Probably no one except this harassed newspaper editor, his head full of political intrigue and his body hoist on an unfamiliar podium, would have noticed it. But to a temporary chairman, the only one looking out at the audience rather than up at the Poet Laureate, it was as clear as a storm.

It seems odd to be writing this now. I have always distrusted the myth of Hughes as master-male, bending others to his whim: so this was not a sight I was searching for. Yes, I was nervous up there on the stage: but, on one glass of warm white wine, I was hardly delirious. I dislike speaking in public: but I had already delivered my chairman's introduction, a brief comparison between the honest pleasure of poetry and the duplicity surrounding a debate that both parties claimed to want but to which neither would commit itself. By the time that Hughes was intoning his Whitman, I was merely looking, impresario-like, to see that the customers were content: and they were well-content, moving sideways and then back as though better to hear the word 'SEX'.

When Hughes was not reading he was sitting next to me at the wooden desk which the organizers had pulled from the Institute of Education store. He curled himself in a prawn posture on his hard-backed chair and waited for his turn at the lectern without, it seemed to me, wholly sitting. I was uncomfortable all the time that he was there. I was relaxed, I confess it, only when his lectern-turn had come and I had a different poet alongside.

While Hughes was with me behind our shared desk Heaney was out there tapping his feet to 'The Ballad of Reading Gaol', an easier poem on the ear than anything of Whitman's and easier almost than anything at all. Yet Heaney's words were not easy to hear. It was as though Hughes were a pile of bricks on my right-hand side.

Let me not exaggerate. This was not a solid wall. His was not a spell of chains. I could easily have broken back out into politics by scribbling notes to my appointments diary for the following day: call Michael Dobbs, the Tory's pop novelist and TV debate coordinator, or procrastinator, as Labour's men see him; fax Peter Mandelson, the man who insists, to Tory snorts, that Tony really wants a debate; fax Derry Irvine to find out if Labour would risk the slightest legal challenge from the Liberal Democrats. I made only a few pointless pencilled marks. To use public politics to escape the private aura around Ted Hughes seemed a deception.

'Song of Myself' is about change and rejuvenation, about what everyone in Britain is thinking now, two weeks before the election. But in Hughes's voice it was about nothing but the poet and the reader, and those, the very grateful, to whom the words were being read. *The Times* has held this sort of forum for hundreds of writers before: the only speaker that came close to Hughes was Mikhail Gorbachev, whom the admirers for some reason did not so much want to hear as to touch.

Out in the audience to the left on the other side from where the wave began, were a small group of colleagues. They had joined the poets, their publishers, Faber and Faber, and our co-hosts, the booksellers Dillons, for a party behind the stage before the reading. A classroom is forever a classroom and there, in the back of the Institute, we all stood like teachers with tumblers in our hands, toasting a colleague off to classrooms new.

The celebration was going with as much of a swing as was ever likely when someone suddenly asked to take a publicity photograph. That required a difficult corralling of Heaney, who was in mid-conversation, of Hughes, who was in mid-quiet, and of the Editor of *The Times*, who was in mid-call to the office about a protest from Labour about some imagined slight. The only people more difficult than the politicians at this time were the broadcasters who, in the words of one Blairite panjandrum, were 'infuriated at *The Times*'s impertinence in attempting to broker a televised debate where they themselves had failed'.

The photographer also wanted the Laureates, as he called them, to hold *The School Bag,* the book which the evening was supposed to promote. Neither the Nobel Laureate nor the Poet Laureate seemed keen to do this: they balanced and bounced it but were reluctant to open their work for any end other than the real one of reading from it. The book came to me and, to the photographer's relief, it fell open: somewhere, anywhere would do.

To add fake verisimilitude of the sort that publicity pictures require I opened my mouth as though speaking. In order to avoid saying anything of my own I stabbed at the first poem on the page: a description of Second World War rifle drill by Henry Reed which baldly began: 'Today we have naming of parts. Yesterday, we had daily cleaning. And tomorrow morning we shall have what to do after firing.'

Heaney and I mumbled about Reed and about how this particular poem was 'one of the most extraordinary works of the war'. Hughes became agitated. 'I hate this poem,' he said as though shovelling rocks into the vacuum around us. 'I once crashed my car while listening to it. That was five or six years ago but I remember: it was that Henry Reed.'

All I could do was to look back down at the page. 'Japonica glistens like coral in all of the neighbouring gardens and today we have naming of parts.' Reed's last line, its recurrent absurdity of rifle-drill and foliage observation, ran silently through my mind as though through my fingers. Hughes hates this poem. The man of hawks and crows and earth, the man who gives animals ideas with his eyes, hates this poem.

But again he drove my thoughts down. The phone rang again in the back of my head: 'You should know,' said my Labour emissary, 'that the Lib Dems are absolutely resolute against your debate.'

Between the party and the reading we waited in the Green Room, a cream room with mirrors and ledges like a rehearsal space for dancers. Hughes's previous link with *The Times* had been his 'Celebratory Pageant' in the paper for the Queen's sixtieth birthday in 1986. We recalled this as we waited for the hall to fill. Hughes recalled to Heaney how he had scribbled it out one morning at immense pace in Heaney's flat, on his kitchen table. There was a lightness in his mood remembering 'The Crown of the Kingdom' that he brought to the mention of nothing else. There seems to be almost nothing public about this Poet Laureate who, as we spoke, was wetting his throat for the last time with champagne from a miniature airline bottle.

Up on stage I spread that poem in front of me on the desk. In my ears there was still a Scottish Labour voice resounding like

[265]

Robert Bruce from the back of a cave and responding to my mention of *The Times*'s legal opinion with the words: 'I hope you don't mind if I prefer my own opinion.'

In 1986, in Hughes's crown of flowers for the Queen were entwined a snowdrop 'her neck bowed watching her modesty', a foxglove 'raggily dressed, long-bodied, a rough blood-rope of dark nipples and full cup' and a daffodil 'whose chill, scrubbed face and cold throat looks utterly true and pure'. Since I could neither concentrate on what Heaney was reading nor on my undone political tasks, I spent the time fitting these flowers to the faces that looked up from the front row.

'Out of the dimness, opposite equals advance, always substance and increase, always sex . . .'

Hughes made Whitman live in his own poet's world. Every one of us heard what Hughes wanted us to hear – and only what Hughes wanted us to hear. This was the only time that I had ever been able to take Whitman seriously. Shame on me but I had always much preferred the public, car-crashing Henry Reed, who looked at the gun and the gardens through the same cold eye and placed them side by side in the same stanza frame.

The evening ended and I left the poets to sign their books for the buyers. On the way to dinner, Michael Dobbs rang from Conservative Central Office. He was even more ill-tempered, suspicious and reminiscent of his own novels' worst characters than before. When I told him that I was just leaving a rather remarkable poetry reading, he became more abrasive still. I was wasting his time. I was not serious. The debate was all a Labour plot.

Then there came the Labour call, saying much the same things. This was not a time for Ted Hughes: the hour of sanity had gone. 'They call it easing the Spring: it is perfectly easy if you have any strength in your thumb, like the bolt and the breech and the cocking piece and the point of balance which in our case we have not got; and the almond blossom silent in all of the gardens, and the bees going backwards and forwards, for today we have naming of parts.'

STEPHEN TABOR

Ted Hughes on the Page

━━━━━

Being one of Ted Hughes's bibliographers – one who studies his books as physical objects – has given me an odd perspective on his work. My concern has not been so much to explicate his words as to trace their transmission in print. This can be useful because a published text inevitably has multiple authors. Editors may have had a hand in the result; typesetters produce accidental variants (sometimes quite plausible ones); designers and illustrators might add their own coloration to a work which each reader will then interpret according to his own personality. One function of bibliography is to try to tease apart these 'contributions' and show how they help or hinder the author's intent.

I can date my bibliographical interest in Hughes to the day a parcel arrived containing a copy of *Prometheus on his Crag*. I had never seen a handmade book before. This fragrant object of purple leather, gold, and deckle-edged paper made somewhere in Italy seemed like a thing I had no business owning. It presented the poetry – some of which I had trouble understanding – with a craftsmanship that demanded my respect as a reader. At the same time it encouraged me to pause along the way and admire what I was seeing. The physical book induced a heightened receptiveness to the nuances of the text. As the punch of the type gave a rough geography to the paper, so the act of reading seemed to take place in a new, more vivid landscape. Since then I have read many hand-printed books, and all of Hughes's poetry as it appeared; but I will never be able properly to assess the Prometheus poems because of that first reading under the best of circumstances.

One could focus in this way on any of more than twenty of Hughes's books that appeared in finely printed limited editions. It was a remarkably consistent record for texts of a living author – thanks in large part to Hughes's sister Olwyn, who brought out much of his work during the 1970s under the Rainbow Press imprint. However, my favourite among these limited editions is the 1973 *Crow,* published by Faber three years after the first trade publication. I try to ignore the outer layers of this book – the slightly discordant colours and slick black spine. Inside is Hughes's most famous collection next to *Birthday Letters,* hand-set from individual sticks of type and printed on fine paper. The designer of both the book and the typeface was Berthold Wolpe, who oversaw the first edition in 1970. The printer, John Roberts Press, was the same small firm that printed the dust-wrapper of the trade printings. The real marvel of this book is the Leonard Baskin drawings, found only in this edition. Like the text, they were printed by pushing metal into paper, and this outmoded technology produced the blackest black possible. Today almost every book is printed by the offset process, which cleverly slides an image of the page onto the paper without making an impression. (To appreciate the difference, compare the colour of Andrew Davidson's wood-engravings in *Tales of the Early World* with that of Baskin's drawings for *Crow.*) Here, every scratch of the pen is faithfully reproduced. In a book pervaded by black, Wolpe and the Roberts Press produced a high point in Hughes's long collaboration with Baskin.

Hughes was lucky to be published from the start of his career by large houses with experienced designers. Many of his trade editions can sit unblushingly on the shelf among their leather-bound relations. (The first printing of *Crow,* for instance, would have been hard to improve upon, at the issue price of £1.) I think the most outstanding of these is Faber's 1995 *Elmet.* These poems are inseparable from Fay Godwin's photographs, from which they took their inspiration. Economies held the first, limited edition (*Remains of Elmet,* 1979) to only four of these photographs, which for technical reasons had to be printed separately from the text and on different paper. The first trade edition, later the same year, put things into balance by including sixty-three photographs and printing them along with the text. Comparing these two versions with *Elmet* is like hearing the poems read by three different voices. But the 1995 design and typography are less stark, more understated, in keeping with Hughes's elimination of several of the more apocalyptic poems. The binding is now full cloth, the colour of Yorkshire slate. Godwin's photographs will probably never be seen to better advantage. The printing took three steps: one to lay down the images in sepia, another to add black to the shadows and print the text, and a third to spread a thin layer of varnish over the illustrations, giving a sparkle which a cheaper production would have got with shiny paper, to the detriment of the reading. The poems and photographs both have a sombre richness; more colour would be out of place here. Set in heavy frames of white, they breathe out the atmosphere of the valley in which Hughes spent the first years of his life.

In singling out these few examples of book-making, I want to urge an occasional indulgence in the sensual side of reading. In a good book, as in a good meal, presentation flatters the contents. There are many chances to enjoy this agreement of sympathies on a shelf of Ted Hughes's books. I invite you to find your favourite, and to reread it with attention to those physical qualities which a computer screen would strip away. With a bit of luck, you could find yourself reading it again for the first time.

TED HUGHES:
A Select Book List

———

with dates of first trade publication

FOR ADULTS

Poetry

The Hawk in the Rain, 1957
Lupercal, 1960
Wodwo, 1967
Crow, 1970
Cave Birds, 1975
Gaudete, 1977
Remains of Elmet, with photographs by Fay Godwin, 1979
Moortown, 1979
River, 1983
Flowers and Insects, 1986
Moortown Diary, 1989
Wolfwatching, 1989
Rain-Charm for the Duchy, 1992
Three Books (*Remains of Elmet, Cave Birds, River*), 1993
Elmet, with photographs by Fay Godwin, 1994
New Selected Poems 1957–1994, 1995
Tales From Ovid, 1997
Birthday Letters, 1998

As editor

A Choice of Emily Dickinson's Verse, 1968
A Choice of Shakespeare's Verse, 1971; revised edition, 1991
A Choice of Coleridge's Verse, 1996
Collected Poems of Sylvia Plath, 1981

The Rattle Bag, with Seamus Heaney, 1982
The School Bag, with Seamus Heaney, 1997

New Versions for Theatre

Oedipus (Seneca), 1969
Spring Awakening (Wedekind), 1995
Blood Wedding (Lorca), 1996
Phèdre (Racine), 1998
The Oresteia (Aeschylus), to be published 1999

Prose

Poetry in the Making, 1967
A Dancer to God, 1992
Shakespeare and the Goddess of Complete Being, 1992
Winter Pollen: Occasional Prose, ed. William Scammell, 1994
Difficulties of a Bridegroom, 1995

FOR CHILDREN

Meet My Folks, 1961
How the Whale Became, 1963
The Earth-Owl and Other Moon People, 1963
Nessie the Mannerless Monster, 1964
The Iron Man, 1968
The Coming of the Kings and Other Plays, 1970
Season Songs, 1974
Moon-Bells, 1978
Under the North Star, 1981
What is the Truth? 1984
Ffangs the Vampire Bat and the Kiss of Truth, 1986
The Cat and the Cuckoo, 1987
Tales of the Early World, 1988
The Iron Woman, 1993
The Dreamfighter and Other Creation Tales, 1995
Collected Animal Poems (Vols 1–4), 1995
Shaggy and Spotty, 1997

For full details of work by and about Ted Hughes see *Ted Hughes: A Bibliography 1946–1995* by Keith Sagar and Stephen Tabor (Mansell, 1998).

Notes on Contributors

A. ALVAREZ is a poet, critic, novelist and author of many books of non-fiction, including *The Savage God*, which includes the first published account of the life and death of Sylvia Plath.

YEHUDA AMICHAI is an Israeli poet. His collection *Amen* (1976) was translated from the Hebrew by the author and Ted Hughes.

SIMON ARMITAGE's collections of poems include *Kid*, *Book of Matches* and *CloudCuckooLand*.

LEONARD BASKIN was born in New Jersey in 1922 and is one of the United States' foremost sculptors. He was a friend of Ted Hughes from the 1950s and collaborated with him on a number of projects, including *Crow* and *Cave Birds*.

MARTIN BOOTH is a novelist, children's author and non-fiction writer.

MELVYN BRAGG is a writer and broadcaster. His novels include *The Maid of Buttermere* and *Credo*.

RAYMOND BRIGGS is an illustrator and artist. His books for children include *The Snowman* and *Father Christmas*. His most recent book, an illustrated memoir of his parents, is *Ethel and Ernest* (1998).

PETER BROOK is Director of the Centre International de Creations Theatrales in Paris. He directed Hughes's adaptation of Seneca's *Oedipus* at the Old Vic in 1968, and staged Hughes's *Orghast* at Persepolis in 1971. His memoir, *Threads of Time*, was published in 1998.

CHARLES CAUSLEY was born in 1917 at Launceston, Cornwall. After serving for six years in the wartime Royal Navy he taught for many years in his home town. His *Collected Poems for Children* was published in 1996 and his *Collected Poems 1951–1997* was published in 1997.

GILLIAN CLARKE is a poet, broadcaster and lecturer on poetry for children. Her collections of poetry include *Five Fields* (1998). Her *Collected Poems* was published in 1997. She lives in Wales.

LINDSAY CLARKE is the author of three novels: *Sunday Whiteman*, *The Chymical Wedding* (which won the 1989 Whitbread Fiction Prize) and *Alice's Masque*.

BARRIE COOKE is an artist, living in Ireland.

WENDY COPE was a full-time teacher for fourteen years, eventually becoming deputy head of a school in the Old Kent Road. When her poems began to be published she went part-time. Soon after the appearance of *Making Cocoa For Kingsley Amis* in 1986 she gave up teaching. Her second collection, *Serious Concerns,* was published in 1992.

ROY DAVIDS is a dealer in, and collector of, manuscripts and literary portraits, and was a friend.

NUALA NÍ DHOMNÁILL's *Selected Poems* were published in 1996.

D. J. ENRIGHT received the Queen's Gold Medal for Poetry in 1981. He was appointed C.Lit. in 1998. His *Collected Poems 1948–98* was published in 1998.

RUTH FAINLIGHT has published books of poems, short stories, translations and libretti. Her sequence of poems *Sibyls*, with woodcuts by the American artist Leonard Baskin, was published in a limited edition by the Gehenna Press in 1991. Her most recent poetry collection, *Sugar-Paper Blue*, was shortlisted for the Whitbread Prize in 1997.

JOHN FOWLES's novels include *The Collector*, *The Magus* and *The French Lieutenant's Woman*.

DONYA FEUER is Director and Choreographer at the Royal Dramatic Theatre, Stockholm, and Professor at the Institute for Education in Stockholm.

SIR JOHN GIELGUD played the title role in Ted Hughes's adaptation of Seneca's *Oedipus*, directed at the Old Vic by Peter Brook in 1968.

TERRY GIFFORD is co-author, with Neil Roberts, of *Ted Hughes: A Critical Study* (1981) and *Green Voices* (1995).

FAY GODWIN is a photographer. Her photographs of the Calder Valley accompany Ted Hughes's poems in *Remains of Elmet* (1979) and the new edition, *Elmet*, published in 1994.

ALAN GOULD is a poet, novelist and essayist living in Canberra, Australia. His recent publications include the poems in *Mermaid* (1996), the collection of essays *The Totem Ship* (1996) and his fifth novel *The Tazyrik Year* (1998). He won the 1992 National Book Council Banjo Award for fiction, and the 1981 New South Wales Premier's Prize for Poetry.

LAVINIA GREENLAW's collections of poetry are *Night Photograph* and *A World Where News Travelled Slowly* (1997).

SEAMUS HEANEY was awarded the Nobel Prize for Literature in 1995. His collection *Opened Ground: Poems 1966–1996* was published in 1998.

SUSAN HILL is a novelist, playwright and publisher.

MICHAEL HOFMANN has published four books of poems with Faber and

Faber, and various translations from the German. He was the co-editor, with James Lasdun, of the volume *After Ovid: New Metamorphoses*, for which four of Ted Hughes's versions were commissioned.

MIROSLAV HOLUB, Czech poet and immunologist, died in 1998 aged seventy-four. His books include *Vanishing Lung Syndrome* and *The Jingle Bell Principle*.

GLYN HUGHES'S first novel, *Where I Used to Play on the Green*, won the Guardian Fiction Prize and the David Higham Award. Later work includes *The Antique Collector*, shortlisted for the Whitbread Fiction Prize, and most recently a novel on the Brontë family, *Brontë*. He has lived the greater part of his life in Ted Hughes's Calder Valley in West Yorkshire.

FRED RUE JACOBS is librarian at Bakersfield College, California, an academic and 'playwright manqué'.

JAMES LASDUN's most recent collection of poetry is *The Revenant* (Jonathan Cape, 1997). He was co-editor, with Michael Hofmann, of *After Ovid: New Metamorphoses*.

R. J. LLOYD is an artist and illustrator living in Devon. He collaborated with Ted Hughes on a number of books including *What is the Truth?* and *The Cat and The Cuckoo*.

ROGER MCGOUGH was born in Liverpool. He has published many collections of poetry for both children and adults. His most recent publications are *The Spotted Unicorn* (1998) and *The Way Things Are* (1999), both published by Penguin.

MEDBH MCGUCKIAN lives in Belfast. Her *Selected Poems* was published in 1997.

JAMIE MCKENDRICK's collection of poetry *The Marble Fly* (Oxford) won the 1997 Forward Prize for Poetry.

LACHLAN MACKINNON is the author of two books of poems, *Monterey Cypress* (1988) and *The Coast of Bohemia* (1991), two works of literary criticism, a biography and frequent book reviews.

W. S. MERWIN, an American poet living in Hawaii, was friends with Ted Hughes since the 1950s. His most recent book is *The Folding Cliffs: A Narrative of 19th Century Hawaii* (Knopf, 1998).

KARL MILLER was editor of the *London Review of Books* from 1979 to 1992 and Professor of English Literature at University College, London, from 1974 to 1992. His memoir *Dark Horses* was published in 1998.

ADRIAN MITCHELL is a poet, playwright and writer of stories for children and adults. He has loved Ted Hughes's work since the 1950s, and was a friend.

MICHAEL MORPURGO is the author of many short stories and novels for children. His most recent publication is *Farm Boy* (1998).

BLAKE MORRISON co-edited *The Penguin Book of Contemporary British*

Poetry. His books include *And When Did You Last see Your Father?*, *The Ballad of the Yorkshire Ripper* and *Too True*, which contains a rare interview with Ted Hughes.

ANDREW MOTION's *Selected Poems 1976–1997* was published in 1998. His biography of John Keats, *Keats*, was published in 1997. He is Professor of Creative Writing at the University of East Anglia.

PAUL MULDOON's most recent collection of poems is *Hay* (1998). His opera libretto *Bandanna* was published earlier this year.

LES MURRAY lives in Australia. He points out he was born on the same day and in the same year as the daredevil motorcyclist Evel Knievel. His poetry is published in the UK by Carcanet, his latest collection being the verse narrative *Fredy Neptune*.

BRIAN PATTEN was born in Liverpool in 1946. He is a poet who writes for both children and adults.

TOM PAULIN is a poet and critic. His collections of critical writing, *Minotaur* and *Writing To The Moment*, both include essays on Ted Hughes.

JILL PIRRIE taught at Halesworth Middle School, Suffolk, where her pupils received national recognition for their poetry writing. Ted Hughes wrote the Foreword to the first edition of her book *On Common Ground*. An anthology of her pupils' poems, *Apple Fire*, was published by Bloodaxe. Now retired, she continues her interest in poetry and education by speaking at teachers' conferences, and writing articles and reviews.

KATHLEEN RAINE has published many collections of poetry and critical essays. She has written on – among others – Coleridge. She is a leading Blake scholar.

PETER REDGROVE's latest collections of poetry are *Assembling a Ghost*, *Orchard End* and *What the Black Mirror Saw*. A new *Selected* is due out in 1999. He lives in Cornwall with his wife Penelope Shuttle. Their most recent joint work is *Alchemy For Women*. Redgrove won the Queen's Gold Medal for poetry in 1996.

CHRISTOPHER REID was poetry editor at Faber and Faber from 1991 to 1999. His collections of poetry include *Expanded Universes*.

KEITH SAGAR, formerly Reader in English Literature at the University of Manchester, is the author of several books on D. H. Lawrence and Ted Hughes, including *The Art of Ted Hughes* (Cambridge University Press, 1978) and, with Stephen Tabor, *Ted Hughes: A Bibliography 1946–1995* (Mansell, 1998). He has just finished a new study of Ted Hughes, *The Laughter of Foxes*.

WILLIAM SCAMMELL edited *Winter Pollen*, a selection of Ted Hughes's occasional prose (Faber, 1994). He is a poet and writes regularly on poetry for the *Independent on Sunday*.

PENELOPE SHUTTLE lives in Cornwall with her husband Peter Redgrove.

Her *Selected Poems* came out in May 1998 from Oxford University Press. She is currently working on a new collection, her seventh, titled *A Leaf Out of His Book*.

ALAN SILLITOE's most recent novel was *The Broken Chariot*, published by Harper Collins.

JON STALLWORTHY's *Rounding the Horn: Collected Poems* and *Singing School*, a fragment of autobiography, were published in 1998. His other books include two critical studies of Yeats's poetry, *The Penguin Book of Love Poetry*, *The Oxford Book of War Poetry*, and two biographies: *Wilfred Owen* (which won the Duff Cooper Memorial Prize, the W. H. Smith Literary Award and the E. M. Forster Award) and *Louis MacNeice* (which won the Southern Arts Literary Prize). He is a Professor of English Literature at Oxford and a Fellow of the British Academy.

PETER STOTHARD is editor of *The Times*.

TIM SUPPLE is artistic director of the Young Vic theatre. He directed the premières of adaptations by Ted Hughes of Wedekind's *Spring Awakening*, Lorca's *Blood Wedding* and Ovid's *Metamorphoses*.

STEPHEN TABOR is the author of *Sylvia Plath: An Analytical Bibliography* (1987) and co-author with Keith Sagar of *Ted Hughes: A Bibliography* (second edition, 1998). He works at the William Andrews Clark Memorial Library of the University of California, Los Angeles.

ADAM THORPE was born in Paris and brought up in India, Cameroon and England. He has published two books of poetry, *Mornings In the Baltic* (1988) and *Meeting Montaigne* (1990), and three novels, *Ulverton* (1992), *Still* (1995) and *Pieces of Light* (1998). His third collection of poems, *From the Neanderthal*, is published by Jonathan Cape in 1999.

ANTHONY THWAITE was born in 1930. He has taught English Literature in universities abroad, has been a literary editor of various journals, and has published thirteen books of poems, most recently *Selected Poems 1956–1996* (1997). His most recent publication is (with Geoffrey Bownas) a revised and expanded *Penguin Book of Japanese Verse* (1998).

CLAIRE TOMALIN was a contemporary of Ted Hughes at Cambridge University, where she read English at Newnham College. Her books include *Jane Austen: A Life* and *The Invisible Woman: The Story of Nelly Ternan and Charles Dickens*

CHARLES TOMLINSON's *Selected Poems 1955–1997* was published in 1997 by Oxford University Press. He lives in Gloucestershire.

MARINA WARNER writes fiction, history and criticism. Her latest book is *No Go the Bogeyman: Scaring, Lulling and Making Mock*, and she is now working on *The Leto Bundle*, a novel.

IRENE WORTH played Jocasta in Ted Hughes's adaptation of Seneca's *Oedipus*, directed by Peter Brook at the Old Vic in 1968.